Praise for *Sales Coaching!*

As the world restructures the way that firms operate towards boundary-less management systems, the role of managers as mentors and coaches becomes imperative. Richardson has developed very powerful and practical coaching techniques for management as well as selling.   *Ian MacMillan, Executive Director*
The Wharton School, University of Pennsylvania

Linda Richardson s techniques are simple, practical, and effective. Even the most seasoned sales managers will find this book an excellent refresher, while newer sales managers will experience *instant* improvement in their coaching effectiveness.
Christine Troianello
Performance Improvement Manager
Lucent Technologies

This is a first-class, quick-reading, practical book for all sales managers.
Ron Galotti, Publisher, Vogue

I have just read *Sales Coaching* for the first time. I say first time because I will read it many more times, as I want to grasp the skills and spiritual part of coaching to practice coaching at the highest level, which is self-coaching. I do not say sales coaching because this book is superb for all types of coaching   *Shigeru Sato*
Consultant, Corporate Marketing and Public Relations
Sumitomo 3M Limited

Sales Coaching can help you make your salespeople more productive even in an environment where time is the scarcest of resources. *Sales Coaching* is the best resource I have read.
Lou Eccleston, Head of Sales, Bloomberg

This book will help you partner with your salesforce to excel together!
Joseph Sparacino, Vice President, CoreStates

With the evolution of the sales process from product to solution and from presentation to consultation, Linda s work is a must read. If you do not embrace Linda s methodology, you will be outsold by those who do!   *David P. Choate*
Senior Vice President
Capital Institutional Services, Inc.

A major league hit. Linda takes the mystery of coaching and turns it into magic for management.   *Josh Hammon, Author*
The Stuff Americans Are Made Of

Successful sales organizations must instill coaching as part of their corporate culture. Linda has created an excellent, practical template for sales coaching with the goal of developing a highly competitive sales team.
Wallace W. Gardner, Jr.
Worldwide Sales Manager
Chubb and Son, Inc.

SALES
COACHING

OTHER BOOKS BY LINDA RICHARDSON

Selling by Phone
Stop Telling, Start Selling

SALES COACHING

Making the Great Leap from Sales Manager to Sales Coach

Linda Richardson

McGraw-Hill

New York   San Francisco   Washington, D.C.   Auckland   Bogot
Caracas   Lisbon   London   Madrid   Mexico City   Milan
Montreal   New Delhi   San Juan   Singapore
Sydney   Tokyo   Toronto

Library of Congress Cataloging-in-Publication Data

Richardson, Linda
    Sales coaching : making the great leap from sales manager to
sales coach / by Linda Richardson.
       p.   cm.
    Includes index.
    ISBN 0-07-052382-7
    1. Sales management. 2. Work groups. I. Title.
    HF5438.4.R46   1996
    658.8'1—dc20   96-22528
                                                  CIP

McGraw-Hill

A Division of The McGraw-Hill Companies

14 15 DOC/DOC 0 9 8 7 6 5 4

ISBN 0-07-052382-7

*The sponsoring editor for this book was Richard Narramore, the
editing supervisor was Caroline Levine, and the production
supervisor was Suzanne W. B. Rapcavage. It was set in Fairfield
by Estelita F. Green of McGraw-Hill's Professional Book Group
composition unit.*

Printed and bound by R. R. Donnelley & Sons Company.

McGraw-Hill books are available at special quantity discounts to
use as premiums and sales promotions, or for use in corporate
training programs. For more information, please write to the
Director of Special Sales, McGraw-Hill, Professional Publishing,
Two Penn Plaza, New York, NY 10121-2298. Or contact your local
bookstore.

This book is printed on recycled, acid-free paper con-
taining a minimum of 50% recycled, de-inked fiber.

watchwords

not boss, but coach
not me, but team
not fear, but support
not words, but behaviors
not closed, but open
not disillusionment
         but
      passion

To the memory of Freddy

Contents

Introduction

Coaching is for everybody, every day. Coaching cannot be relegated only to quarterly, monthly, or even weekly "sessions" (which, by the way, almost no one makes time for). Although more formal coaching sessions remain important, they are only one part of coaching. The goal of this book is to help a manager make the leap from boss to coach by learning how to provide developmental coaching as a part of everyday contact. Becoming a coach begins with the manager understanding the coaching process and using it to move salespeople to self and peer coaching—so that everyone on the team becomes a coach.

This book shows why and how to create a sales coaching culture that results in a top-performing and cohesive sales force that can *coach itself.* The book shows how a *sales manager* can transform him- or herself into a *sales coach* and then help transform others—helping them make the journey from ordinary to extraordinary as they take responsibility for their own development.

Everyone has a fear of being seen as wrong. Yet, especially with today's complexities, no one can know and do everything. In the words of Lao-Tsu, "To know that you do not know is the best." Developmental coaching offers a process that helps coaches and salespeople *enjoy* getting better in what is important in their lives. It allows salespeople to recognize and accept where they are, yet work in a focused way to get to their next level—and the level after that. Developmental coaching encourages a vision of excellence and fosters a passion to achieve excellence continually and incrementally.

Almost everyone in business today understands that there are two kinds of leadership: old leadership and new leadership. Simply put, old leadership was based on controlling people. New leadership is based on empowering people so they can be as good as they can be. In the new leadership the idea is to manage without micromanaging. To do this requires coaching—the most critical competitive skill any organization can have. Unfortunately, however, it is a skill most managers have not acquired, much less mastered.

The Power of Coaching

Leadership today is about vision. It is about understanding the past to make the future better. There are two ways to get better: work harder and/or change. Coaching is about how to change by doing things differently. Every organization and person has blind spots. The power of coaching lies in turning those blind spots into perspective. An organization's people are one of its most important assets. If its people are not improving every day as a way to reach their potential, the company can not fully benefit from their talents.

An organization literally leaves money on the table when there is no coaching among managers and peers. This "money" comes in the form of energy, creativity, ideas, skill, and talent, as well as hard cash. Every organization and manager knows hiring and firing are expensive and that developing people is a much more effective way to realize more potential from its people.

People often draw an analogy between coaching in sports and corporate coaching. And because of this, the word *coaching* is generally accepted (unlike "softer" words such as *mentoring*, *empowering*, and *counseling*). Just as a player has to compete to get on a team in sports, a salesperson has to compete to get his or her job. But for most organizations, this is where the comparison ends. Leadership without coaching is like owning a sports team without trying to make it better. Coaching by the manager can help the team play better, and coaching by the players themselves can help the team play its best.

Most of the salespeople we work with tell us they are hungry for coaching and feedback, but they say they don't get this—they don't get feedback on how they are doing—unless it is to tell them they are doing something wrong.

Most coaching comes in the form of telling or evaluating, not questioning and developing. If you ask a salesperson when was the last time he or she got real coaching, you are apt to get a blank stare. The sad part, and at the same time the best part, of all this is that *most* managers want to help. Most of the managers we work with express a desire to coach. But invariably they also express doubts about their ability to coach. One manager expressed what many feel when he said, "I'm wondering if what I do when I 'coach' is really coaching."

The Standoff

Many managers intellectually recognize the bottom-line impact coaching can have. Most are acutely aware that in today's business environment differentiating the quality of service (including sales quality) is easier than differentiating products—and that even if products can be differentiated, companies need salespeople as a competitive edge. Yet there is a greater standoff today in the workplace: Everybody is waiting for somebody else to do something. Salespeople complain that their managers don't take initiative; managers have the same complaint about salespeople.

The manager is in a great spot to *initiate* the shift to true coaching by changing the dynamic of how he or she works with his or her people.

The Big Hurdle

Much harder than teaching managers *how to* coach is helping managers *want* to coach. The job is a lot easier if senior management is on board:

- Does senior management compensate for and reward coaching?
- Does senior management value coaching?
- Does senior management allow the time for coaching?
- Does senior management provide the skills training for coaching?

But the most important question is, *does senior management coach?* This is the true dividing line between the old management and the new leadership.

If senior management shows *through action* that it truly values coaching, then coaching can become a way of life in the organization. Fortunately, even when this does not happen, *one* manager can make the change—at least for her or his team.

Wasteland

The critical importance of coaching a salesforce is universally acknowledged—as is its almost total absence. Sales coaching is the wasteland of corporate America.

Many people have the title "sales *manager,*" but how many coach? How many receive coaching from *their* managers? I have asked these questions for 15 years. More specifically, for the past 4 years I have asked these questions at the beginning of my *Perspectives in Salesforce Management Seminar* at the Wharton Executive Development Center to senior level national sales managers from corporations and institutions around the world.

I can't recall hearing of an organization where coaching is a way of life. And only once—in the spring 1994 session—did a participant acknowledge that he *got* coached. When asked what he attributed this to, he said (pointing across the room), "Because my boss is sitting over there." His response provoked laughter, perhaps because his honesty was so refreshing—but his answer was sad, and all too true. According to a recent (late 1995) poll by Personnel Decisions International in Minneapolis, Minnesota, 9 of 10 employees want job coaching, but only 4 out of 10 receive it consistently.* In the sales arena, the level may be even lower. And often when managers "coach," what they are actually doing most of the time is not coaching but rather evaluation or assessment.

Every organization we talk with wants to develop a proactive salesforce. They say they want coaching for their salespeople. Yet creating a coaching culture remains elusive to many of them.

Organizations know they need coaching to achieve a competitive advantage in a fast-changing and challenging marketplace. Why is it then that so few do it? More important, how can they do it?

First, organizations can make feedback the norm for how people work. The companies and coaches who can do this will win; those who can't will lose. Even if an organization has a compelling vision, even if it is highly marketing-oriented, and even if it has sales systems, without developmental coaching as a way of life and feedback as a mainstay of communication, its management

---

*Item entitled "Buddy System" in the "Work Week" column of *The Wall Street Journal*, December 12, 1995, p. 1-A1.

and salespeople cannot *continuously* improve and get to the next level *fast* enough.

Coaching as approached in this book is not about long, laborious coaching sessions. It's about taking the time to help salespeople become responsible for their own development. It is a quick, helpful exchange for 2 to 5 minutes during the action as well as in half hour or so sit-down sessions.

Becoming a sales coach makes being "the boss"—the evaluator—part a lot easier. It makes it more fun. And most of all, it makes everybody, including the coach, a better sales professional.

The kind of coaching covered in this book is developmental. *Developmental coaching* begins with a higher dependency on the coach. The better the coach and the more coaching he or she does, the less the dependency on the coach. As the term *developmental* suggests, this coaching is an incremental process of helping people get to their next level of growth. The power of developmental coaching is that it does more than help a salesperson remove a particular obstacle. As it does so, it teaches the salesperson *the process of removing other obstacles him or herself.* The more effective the coaching, the less the coach is needed. And when coaching leads to self and peer coaching as an everyday occurrence, the coaching process truly takes root.

Clearly, sales coaching is a Herculean task. Not only are there very few role models, but many organizations lack the environment needed for coaching to germinate, let alone thrive. In some companies, there is a natural bias against real coaching.

This book focuses on what one coach can do to transform an organization. Rather than only giving sales managers a finish line to cross, it shows them how to make each day a new beginning—one in which they and their people continuously get better and better to win.

Coach versus Boss
—the Mindset

Sales managers today face unprecedented change. Whether the change involves technology, organizational strategy, or product development, it is really about only one thing: finding new ways to serve customers and making those ways work. As a result of this development, now, for the first time, *sales managers*, not senior managers, are the focal point of change.

Traditionally in companies senior management makes all the decisions and calls all the shots. But top-down leadership does not work in today's environment of rapid change. Too many opportunities perish when a few individuals in *isolation* at the top lead the organization. Top-down management does work when you have to do the same thing year after year and can repeat successful patterns from the past. But a company has to adjust to change—from both the inside and the outside. A company needs to be in close touch with its environment, both internal and external. Effective sales managers today are in the right place to make the inside-outside connection. They are out in the field, near the customer. Yet they are also on the inside track, linking the sales force to top management.

The cover story of the October 1994 issue of *Sales & Marketing Magazine* predicted the "Death of a Sales Manager." William Keenan, managing editor, blamed the demise of the traditional sales manager role on six factors: communication, technology, sales force automation, empowerment, team selling, and customer focus. But Keenan's daring title was more of a wake-up call than a funeral announcement. The sales manager role is not disappearing—it is reemerging. It is being transformed into a new and vital role—from evaluator to developer, from expert to resource, from teller to questioner. This change is no mere tweaking adjustment—it is a 180-degree shift from how most sales managers manage and how they are managed.

Most organizations profess to want coaching, but they don't really do anything about it. Just as students are lucky to have one or two special teachers in a lifetime, most sales professionals are lucky if they get *one* real coach! Organizations don't have role models for coaching, they don't train for it, and they don't hold people accountable for it. In the companies where managers *do* attempt to coach, they can be sabotaged. In one company a powerful producer—"protected by the chairman"—continuously undermined her manager's efforts to create a team culture and would only begrudgingly "allow" her junior sales associate to sit next to her to observe and hear phone calls if he agreed to not utter a word before or after the calls!

Almost every major company wants to "partner" with its clients. But this is impossible if the company cannot partner inside its own walls first, because internal competition and distrust are the enemies of cross-leveraging. Going from "boss" to "coach" is the way to achieve partnering inside, by fostering internal communication and teamwork. And inside partnering is a powerful advantage not easily copied by competitors.

One sales manager in a company that is number one in its field told us that throughout his industry he sees a "vintage" of midcareer professionals from the transaction-based 1980s who "don't know how to coach" and younger salespeople behind them who "are demanding coaching" now. "They all need to learn about coaching—how to give it and how to receive it. *If we can accomplish this in our organization, we can differentiate ourselves from our competition."*

Think about your own organization. If you had to sketch it for your neighbor, what would you draw? Probably a pyramid or a triangle, the ultimate symbol of hierarchy. Or maybe you would design a complex organizational chart. What does the traditional pyramid or organizational chart tell you about? It tells you about the structure and hierarchy of the *company.* It doesn't tell anything about the needs of the *customers,* strengths and weaknesses of the *competition,* or the nature of the *environment.*

The organizational charts that *most* companies use are *internal maps,* not external ones, and almost always the people closest to the customer occupy the lowest echelons of the chart, *if they appear at all.* The game of hierarchy clearly is to get to the top—and as organizations flatten, this is an ever-narrowing, competitive top. Hierarchies, with their inherent "boss-subordinate" structure, inevitably generate superior-subordinate relationships rather than collegial ones, precluding easy introduction of internal partnering, teaming, or coaching.

Because of this, the culture of most organizations is *counter-coaching.* A sales manager I greatly admire—one of the few sales *coaches* at work today—said that he loved this book, but he had one major concern. The real question, he said, was: Why should managers want to coach? If you think about it, you have to admit he is right. Why *should* anyone playing hierarchy really help someone else? Coaching skills alone—although very important—won't change a "boss" into a coach. The skill part of coaching is the *easy* part—and we will get to that soon. But much more than any set of skills is the mindset.

The hierarchy is not going away, and I am *not* suggesting that it should. It is *not* the structure of an organization that blocks coaching; it is its *spirit.* Coaching is first a philosophy, a way of life. It is mental. It is spiritual. It is visceral—a gut-level attitude that determines how a manager works with his or her people. The good news is that the coaching "spirit" can begin with a single manager. A manager can live in a hierarchy and change the dynamic of how she or he works with people. And changing the dynamic will produce bottom-line gains for the organizations that can do it.

If sales managers wait for senior management to initiate the change, they may have a long wait. The people at the top, more often than not, are usually *not* the ones to promote coaching, even if they support it. And even when top management is committed to coaching, the people directly "under" them, often in fierce competition for the pinnacle position, are normally not interested in changing the game at this stage in their careers. The changes from boss to coach can start with one manager. It is up to managers to change how they think about their jobs and how they interact with their people.

What does it mean to coach? One manager rated himself a great coach. Why? He said, "My door is always open. My people know they can come to me when they need me." Certainly this manager might be a very effective coach when the opportunity *presents itself,* but this responsive mode is only one small part of coaching.

What is your mindset? What words would you choose to describe yourself as a manager? What would you use as synonyms for *manager?* Think about the terms you chose. Do they describe a hierarchical structure such as *boss* or *supervisor,* or did you choose more collaborative words such as *coach, colleague, partner,* or *teammate?*

How do you see your role in relation to others? How much time do you spend "doing" (player/producer) versus "coaching" (model/mentor)? How important to you is it to be a player versus a coach? What are you rewarded for? What is your attitude about developing your people? Is it part of your job? How much feedback do you give? How much feedback do you get? How are you managed? Who coaches you?

Why Coach?

Why bother to coach? Because without coaching you and your people will not change fast enough in today's fast-paced, competitive world. Because with it you will continuously improve and become more effective and more competitive. Coaching skills will help you lead your people and love your job. Moreover, coaching skills are transferable from work life to personal life.

One of the top financial organizations in the world, renowned for its culture and profitability, set as its 1996 goal two objectives: "stay on top" (it is number one in its field) and "keep the team together." The plan to keep the team together involved investing in and coaching teams and team members. This firm knew that the team coaching is the doorway to real empowerment and continuous improvement for the coach, the team, and the organization. They knew coaching would help managers and teams adapt to a fast-changing environment and will help them produce better results.

As mentioned earlier, everyone has blind spots—areas too close to perceive completely or clearly. To see a full, sharp picture, every individual needs an outside view. And that is why everyone needs coaching and feedback. Coaching is a process of helping people get to their next level of excellence by helping them understand and overcome their obstacles. Coaching opens perspectives—for both the person being coached and the coach. It is a process that empowers people to accomplish great things.

It is not unusual for corporate eyes to roll when the word

empowerment is mentioned. One major organization, professing to be committed to teams, levied a $1.00 fine for anyone using the "E" word (empowerment). Whereas a large number of organizations today may acknowledge the importance of coaching and even restructure to create coaching roles, the people leading these initiatives often view coaching as "soft." This attitude was clearly evident in a January 23, 1994, *New York Times* article in which Joe Montana's style of management was described as "contradicting" the 1990s ideal of "a consensus-oriented team builder who *gently listens and empowers.*" The management specialist in the article said, "These aren't touchy-feely executives; they tell the troops what the hell they want." The assumption here is that if you do not tell—"boss"—the troops, you are a touchy-feely, consensus-oriented team builder who is weaker and less effective. The opposite of telling the troops what they want, in this view, is tantamount to a "love in." In this world "real" managers don't coach, they boss. This book is about coaching by asking, not coaching by telling.

Certainly there is no substitute for being clear on expectations and goals. Being a good coach does not mean a lack of clarity or direction. Of course there are times to tell—for example, an urgent situation or a highly critical one. But when developing a person is your goal, you can meet it only by coaching.

While there is a "soft" side to coaching, it is soft where it should be soft—on people. There is also a hard side to coaching that is hard where it should be hard—on accountability. There is a time to develop and a time to evaluate. And not necessarily simultaneously. Today, soft is hard. Soft skills are to hard skills as software is to hardware.

The goal of empowering people is the same as the goal of parenting—to help people become independent. When managers tell people what to do—"tell the troops what the hell they want"—

they thwart independence. Just as there are times when it is necessary to call the shots, there are also many times for team input. Sunday may be the time to shout and set up plays, but what happens the other six days will impact how well the plays are executed before the next "game."

When people are involved, they generate their own motivation. They, not external forces such as the carrot (reward) or the stick (punishment), are the motivators. They buy in. They are turned on. Rather than the carrot or the stick being the generators, their internal drive is the generator.

While organizations do put significant talent and dollars to create sales management roles, most of the time the emphasis is on measurement and evaluation, *not* development.

There is a trend today for the manager to play the role of a player/coach. Certainly this can be an excellent model. It creates good role models, it increases credibility, it ensures that managers stay close to the market, and it allows managers to try out new programs and products. The only problem is that the "player" role can shortchange or eclipse the coaching role.

Why Managers Don't Coach

When sales managers are asked why they don't coach, they usually say it is because they don't have the time. Looking at the workload of today's managers, the "no time" obstacle rings true. Coaching does take time, especially for the player/coach, who must focus on his or her own business as well as coach. In the short run, coaching takes more time than not coaching. And "real coaching"—what we refer to as developmental coaching—can take more time than "one-minute" coaching (saying, "Good catch but here's what's wrong and here's what to do"). Such "triage" coaching does make sense in emergencies—but not as a way of life. But despite the time pressures, our experience with thousands of managers shows that time is not the primary reason they don't coach.

In our management seminars, we frequently ask sales managers to think about a salesperson on their team who is overdue for feedback for a sales problem. Immediately, each sales manager can identify someone. We then ask how long the problem has been going on. Participants grin and squirm. Why? Often the problem has been going for weeks or months. As we discuss this, many of the would-be coaches acknowledge they are *avoiding* the problem for reasons they can all articulate—they don't feel comfortable, they are really not expected to coach, they want to avoid confrontation, they don't want to damage the relationship, they don't know what to do.

My experience of over 18 years with literally thousands of sales managers and salespeople across industries leads me to believe that there are three overriding reasons why most managers don't coach:

- They themselves are not coached (no role models). The culture does not support coaching.

- They don't know how to coach (no skill).

- They have little or no incentive or accountability to coach—no inspiration or motivation (no will).

Of these three reasons, the first is the most serious; the second, lack of training, is the easiest to fix. Sales managers are rarely trained to carry out the management part of their role. Managers are basically "knighted," not trained. Almost invariably, they get their jobs because they are the top performers. There is nothing wrong with this. But these doers like to do. Certainly *in the short run* doing takes less time and has fewer risks. Moreover, traditionally, the qualities that contribute to managers' own successes can't be the antithesis of what it takes to be a developer of others. The problem is that when these "star" salespeople are promoted, they usually continue to do what they did best—perform more as solo players than team builders. Mind set and skill set training can help this.

A real obstacle to coaching is the culture of an organization. One manager we spoke with said, "I understand you want to talk to me about the 'C' word." Our short discussion with him revealed he did not like things that are "soft" (meaning unimportant). He went on to say that a coaching session in his organization meant that "You are in trouble."

"Do Not Enter"—What Every Coach Needs to Know about Zones

One of the main obstacles to effective coaching can be territorial in nature. Sometimes the coach, the organization, or the person to be coached is in the wrong "space" for coaching. We have a word for cultural space: *zone.*

When people think about their jobs, they often think in terms of roles, skills, and competencies. Although these things are all very important in understanding *what* people do, it is essential to stop and take a look at how people approach their jobs and also their lives. One way to take a step back and find out where people are "coming from" is to understand the *culture zones* a person, a team, or an organization is living in.

We define four zones: the Dead Zone, the Comfort Zone, the Stretch Zone, and the Panic Zone. Everyone lives and works— usually in that order—predominantly in *one* zone. Certainly, there is movement back and forth, but most people stabilize in one place—at least for a period.

In which zone do you think people learn best, in the Dead, Comfort, Stretch, or Panic Zone?

Some people believe that they and others learn and produce best in the Panic Zone—including the top management of some multinational companies. They try to put and keep people in the Panic Zone because they believe that is where productivity will be the highest. One multinational company that believes this is very profitable, but it is also known for a culture driven by fear. Its distinction for 1995 was having the highest turnover at *all* levels in its industry. How much more profitable could this company be if it could develop and retain its best people?

Others believe that people learn and produce best in the Comfort Zone because that is where people don't feel threatened and, therefore, can be more effective and productive. This view is also off. We all know the corporate giants that stabilized in the Comfort Zone.

Let's get inside each of these four zones to understand where learning happens best.

The Dead Zone

People who live here are not actively interested in improving. They take no initiative to get better. *People here stay the same.* They do not seek the things that make them change. Typically they are people to whom *things happen.* Of these people one can say, "They retired years ago..." even when they are still working at their jobs! People in the Dead Zone have stopped improving. They have stopped trying. They are resigned to things *as they are,* and more important, *as they were.* They seek confirmation for their past and present. They lack interest in the future. They are disengaged.

The Comfort Zone

In contrast to people in the Dead Zone, people in the Comfort Zone *want* to be effective. They have been successful in the past and want to continue to be so, so they do the same old things that worked before. This zone is very seductive because it is natural for people to reproduce what made them successful in the past. Unfortunately, they make a dangerous assumption: they fail to see that everything in their world continues to change—everything but them. They *fine-tune* in response to change but *they* don't change.

People and organizations in the Comfort Zone think of themselves as open, but they really are not. The people living here may be smart and work hard, but they have blinders on—and they do not get the feedback or support necessary to help them *see around their blinders and progress beyond the Comfort Zone.*

The Panic Zone

A lot of people spend a lot of time here. This is the zone of reactive adjustment. What's good about the Panic Zone is that it wakes people up and gets their attention. People here care very much or they wouldn't panic. But because they feel panicked, they can't learn well or perform well here. Their judgment is impaired. They *do not* make good decisions. Burnout happens here. Quality suffers. People are pushed into indecision. People here don't feel competent to handle what is before them. In extreme cases a person can become paralyzed. One client, when confronted with the concept of zones, said, "I have a fifth—the Depression Zone." This was understandable. During our meeting the boss of this highly competent sales manager came in and reamed him out. The organization was in the Panic Zone all right, moving into depression. Another client described her organization's zone as the War Zone, and articles in the press over the next month told why.

Life is no fun in the Panic Zone. Some people and organizations say they operate best in the Panic Zone, but when they are asked to look at what they mean by "panic," they usually talk about the exhilaration and excitement connected with the energy that they feel. This is quite different from panic or depression. In the long run panic does not give energy, it takes it. It *creates exhaustion—diminishing and draining everyone.* Think about the Olympic skater who could do a triple-axel jump yesterday but not today.

People in the Panic Zone know the old systems aren't working, but they are often at a loss as to what to do about that. They often blame their organizations, not themselves. They do not feel in control. How can they regain control? The solution is in them. *Winding up in the Panic Zone is the result of being in the Comfort Zone too long.* This can be as short as a few weeks or as long as a few months—not years.

The Stretch Zone

The Stretch Zone is entirely different from any of these zones. It is a good place to live and work. People in the Stretch Zone are actively involved in their work and are committed to developing themselves. They are looking to change in a major way. They actively seek to *do things differently.* They say to themselves, "Although I have been successful, I will *intentionally* do things differently to at least stay in sync with change." Unlike those in the Dead Zone, people in this zone do not feel threatened by change. They see it as an opportunity. They believe that they can control their destiny by their actions and approach. People who are committed to the Stretch Zone understand they have blind spots and that they *must* be open to feedback to compensate for them.

We believe that most individuals learn best in the Stretch Zone. In the Dead Zone and Comfort Zone, life is too comfortable. There are no new challenges, so there are few new opportunities to learn. In the Panic Zone, there is usually too much fear to learn anything. In the Depression or War Zone, people are in pain. In the Stretch Zone, incremental, planned development offers the best opportunity for growth—a step at a time, continuously moving forward, stretching without breaking. Stretch is a model of potential—because no one ever gets to the outer parameter. People are *always* changing and improving. There is *always* room to get better.

Most people won't dispute that Stretch is the best zone to live and work in. So why isn't there more living and working in this zone?

The problem with the Stretch Zone is that it is hard to be there all the time, especially all alone. Fortunately, people do not have to be there alone. They can be a part of a team. The invention or dynamic of the team allows a person to get and stay in Stretch most of the time. The deal among team members is that they will help each other around their blinders. The space needed for the Stretch Zone is a space of support, not fear. A coach can be the catalyst to change the zone from Comfort to Stretch.

The key is that individuals as well as organizations can bring zones into play. So in thinking about zones, check *your* zone, not just the zone of your organization.

Where Is Your Zone?

The open question for your life and your work is which zone do you want to be in? More important, why? Where do you want your sales and support people to be? If it is the Stretch Zone, then how do you and each of your people get in and stay there? How can you arrange or configure your group to increase the odds of getting and staying in the Stretch Zone, where developmental coaching can occur? The coach can move toward "Stretch" by changing how he or she works with each of his or her salespeople.

A Team of Two

A basic team has two people, and it expands from there. Developmental sales coaching is all about creating the basic team of two—the sales coach and the salesperson. When the sales coach and salesperson feel as though they are on a team together, they can make things happen.

Many organizations are moving toward teams. Some are even basing managers' compensation on team performance. Later in this book we will look at team coaching. But this comes last because it requires an important fundamental: Teams can't be effective unless there is one-on-one trust and positive relationships. Team members work best when they work as peers who trust each other. A real team is formed when the goal of the team becomes more important than the individual's goal. That's exactly what Brown meant when he said before the 1996 Super Bowl that he only cared about winning the game, "not personal achievement."

Critical Success Factors of Coaching

Webster's New World Dictionary (third edition) defines the noun *coach* as "an instructor or trainer," with the verb *to coach* meaning to "instruct or to train." But what does this really mean on the job?

We have asked hundreds of managers for their ideas about what it takes to be a really effective sales coach. Specifically, we have asked them to come up with what they consider to be the four or five critical success factors for successful coaching. We define *critical success factors* as the *few* key elements that can have the greatest impact on results and without which success cannot be achieved. This is what we are told over and over:

- *Role modeling.*   The coach lives the vision.

- *Trustworthiness.* The coach has earned the trust of his or her people.

- *Mutual respect.* The coach respects and is respected; it is a two-way street. The coach lets *you* figure it out.

- *Communication.* The coach has good communication skills.

- *Experience/value added.* The coach has relevant experience that allows him or her to add value.

- *Praise.* The coach gives positive feedback.

We also asked managers to identify the critical success factors of being a boss. Not too many people were at a loss for this. They said things like the "guy/gal upstairs" who *tells* you what to do. Here's a typical set of critical success factors that they describe for a boss:

- Title

- Power

- Position

- Authority

- Status

Webster defines *boss* as person "in authority over employees." The verb *to boss* has a pejorative connotation: "to order about," as in "Do this. Do that."

Each manager needs to decide which operation—boss or coach—is right for him or her and which will lead to the best results. Managers need to understand when to boss and when to coach—and, as coaches, when and how to evaluate and when and how to develop. Knowing which "culture zone" you are in— and which zone you want to be in—can help you make this choice and can help your salespeople be ready for coaching.

Attitudes

Of course, many organizations and managers are committed to training and development and spearhead and participate in it. But language tells a lot about how organizations and managers feel about coaching. Expressions like "sink or swim" or "shape up or ship out" reveal cultures that oppose training. In many organizations and among some managers, there is the prevailing attitude that the need for training is a sign of weakness. One manager described his organizational culture as "survival of the fittest."

By contrast, it is impossible to find even one common business saying that reinforces development and support. "Blossom and grow" is hardly a corporate expression. One frustrated training manager entitled his training plan, in quotation marks, "Important but Not Essential" to spotlight the prevailing attitude and the resulting mediocre, outdated training that his company provided. His cynicism was his way of coping with a lip-service approach to development.

I experienced the most extreme example of negativity toward training when I was training a group of salespeople a number of years ago. One young man was fired up with enthusiasm about the feedback and ideas he was getting in the sales training—that is until the break. When he returned he was crestfallen and solemn. At the next break I asked him if something was wrong. He looked at me with resentment and said, "I just saw X (a senior officer of the firm), and he asked me where I was going. I said, 'To sales training.'" The young man went on to say that as the elevator door closed the senior said, "If you need sales training, you shouldn't be here!"

For training to have impact, managers must support and role-model it. The coach has to be involved from the start to influence the training and inspire participation, in the middle to cheerlead and participate in it, and, most important, at the end to reinforce it. The manager is the key to how people view training and what they get out of it. When salespeople are negative about the sales training they are given, for example, there is a strong probability something is wrong with it (not relevant, not challenging, not credible, not interactive, etc.) or there may be something wrong with the attitude of the people. In either case, it is the role of the manager to get feedback and be a part of the solution, not the problem.

From Boss to Coach

Of course, when a manager is part of an organization that values coaching, it is easier for him or her to make the transition from boss to coach. Fortunately, however, without that, *all* it takes is *initiative—doing it.*

As mentioned earlier, managers who want to change from boss to coach can initiate the change themselves. They don't have to wait for approval from above. They don't have to wait for changes in the structure or hierarchy of the organization. They can start immediately by changing the *dynamics* of how they work with their own people, their own managers, and people in other divisions. They can create a behavioral—not structural—hierarchy of peers.

To understand the difference between the structure and the dynamics of a situation, think about a person who reports to you now and with whom you have a great working relationship. How do you work with this person—as a boss or as a peer? The answer is probably peer. The reporting structure may be that of "boss/subordinate," but the relationship is that of "peer/team."

This example illustrates the tremendous importance of culture in training. Indeed, as committed as our company is to training, we recognize that training really doesn't train. It only opens the book. It enhances awareness, and creates a framework and common language so people can learn and improve as they work, if the culture allows it. Whatever a company's culture is, that is the true teacher. Culture trains.

The sales manager is in a unique position to become a catalyst for change. She or he is in the right spot to see the adjustments that have to be made and to help people make these adjustments. Making the journey from boss to coach means placing the primary responsibility for learning *not* in training seminars but directly in the hands of the coach and his or her people. This makes "training" and learning an *everyday* activity rather than an event. It shifts the job of training from the "preachers" to the "practitioners." The coach and his or her people should continuously assess their own strengths— salesperson to salesperson as well as coach to salesperson—and give feedback on what formal training programs they need as their jumpstart. When this happens, people become responsible for their own learning, and they can grow and expand their capabilities daily. Formal sales and strategy training help accelerate this learning process by providing a framework, establishing a common language, and setting the skill development in motion.

One new senior manager (we'll call him Frank) faced a team of salespeople who, while they were high performers, had been schooled under the previous manager to act in a totally dependent way. The solution to any challenge or problem that was even slightly important was "Ask Frank!" For example, Frank's people used to check all pricing with him all the time. Through developmental coaching with each of his people, he helped *empower* them to handle most of the pricing situations that previously found their way to his door. Working with strategic pricing guidelines set by management, he empowered his team.

Frank helped his salespeople learn how to effectively negotiate themselves. He provided a negotiation training program tailored to his people and participated in their training. He then set up a coaching program to help build their skills. By increasing his people's skill and knowledge and helping to change their attitudes, he fostered their independence and success. He also strengthened his relationship with them. Best of all he helped his company realize a pricing policy that was vital to its relationship strategy and profitability.

Frank linked formal training with ongoing coaching. He understood that *culture trains.* The culture of an organization is the everyday practices of the management of the organization. Culture is what management does, not what it says. Training can support the culture; it usually cannot change it. Culture is stronger than skills. That is why the role of the coach is vitally important. Frank was there as a role model and reinforcer, and he gained maximum impact from the training.

Creating a Coaching Culture

The best news in all this is that to be an effective coach—even in a culture that appears to be anticoaching—takes only one thing: *you.* It can start with one coach, one unit, one division, one team—or any two people who are ready to change *how they work together.*

The shift toward coaching can begin with a coach who changes the *dynamic* of how he or she or the team members work together and with others. A procoaching attitude can be contagious person to person and eventually team to team and unit to unit. As mentioned, creating a coaching culture does not require changes to organizational structure. In fact, structural changes intended to improve cultures can actually worsen them. Many companies have "flattened" the pyramid, only to make their environments even more competitive and fearful. It is important to know: Are the managers coaches or bosses, supporters or antagonists, team players or lone stars, developers or evaluators?

Coaches must figure out what factors are in their control and work on them. Does the coach have the power to influence management, evaluative, and/or compensation systems to support coaching? If so, good. If not, coaches can still have an impact. As they do this, they often find far fewer limitations than expected. Even in a worst-case scenario—a Dead Zone or Panic Zone situation—a coach can make a difference in his or her own sphere with his or her own people by changing the zone. The deal is one that starts between coach and salesperson. The coach is committed to helping the salesperson reach his or her next level. The salesperson is open to this. This kind of behavior doesn't happen in the Panic Zone. It does not happen when people are afraid or when there is destructive internal competition. Nor does it happen in the Dead or Comfort Zone. It thrives in the Stretch Zone, where there is openness to cooperation and change. Managers who want to move from boss to coach can begin with their own group to create an environment in which peers are committed to helping each other—a climate of support, not fear; of teamwork, not internal competition.

Unfortunately, what most managers do when they "coach" is evaluate, not develop their people to help them become independent. The challenge is to increase the time managers spend coaching and decrease the time spent evaluating.

Two Kinds of Feedback

The key to both change and cooperation is *feedback,* a term that has become a part of business language of the 1990s. Previously, the term was heard only in areas such as human resources. For anyone standing in line at a train station or waiting in an airport, it is not unusual today to overhear a businessperson use this term, as in: "Well, we'll see if he accepts the feedback. If not, there will be...." In organizations where coaching is becoming a way of life—where managers and peers give feedback—people increase their effectiveness.

What is feedback? *Feedback is the process of giving data to someone about the impact the person makes through his or her attitudes, actions, and words.* If there is lots of honest, open feedback going on in an organization, up and down and sideways, that is a clear signal that the environment is in the Stretch Zone and that people are learning and changing.

Unfortunately, this is not the case; most people dread feedback. They often react negatively, both physically (heart pounding, dry throat) and mentally (fearful, nervous, defensive), when they hear they are going to give or worse get feedback. They anticipate criticism, and they feel they will be under attack. Ego goes up and receptivity goes down. This is because people look at feedback as evaluative, not developmental—probably because that is how they have experienced it. The word *feedback* itself might be part of the problem. It sounds clinical. In addition to this, negative feelings are often passed on directly or indirectly by managers who themselves are not comfortable giving or getting feedback. *But the main reason feedback is looked upon negatively is that the person receiving the feedback believes the feedback is judgmental and that the motives of the giver may be negative.* People are not accustomed to feedback as a form of ongoing development. Without a basis of trust, good feedback probably won't be given. If it is, it won't be well received.

Although many people try to avoid getting feedback initially (and resent it mightily when they do get it if they don't trust the giver), once a person experiences *good* feedback aimed at helping him or her get to the next level—*developmental* feedback—*he or she becomes hungry for more.* It is not unusual after our sales seminar in which people taste intensive, individual feedback, that they express resentment at their organizations for not having given them feedback before. These are the people who begin to demand feedback and development.

The vast majority of the participants who attend our seminars identify the individual feedback they get in our training as the most valuable part of the training. What makes this response even more impressive is that this feedback is given by the trainer and peers in the presence of peers, not one-on-one. And most of these participants, when asked for the type of reinforcement they want from the training, ask for the opportunity to get *more* feedback.

But we should not kid ourselves. Regardless of how positive participants are about feedback given in the seminar, seminars are seminars. They do not occur every day. Unless the manager buys in, feedback cannot become a part of the culture outside the seminar room. That means development stays *in* the seminar room. The enthusiasm for feedback will come to an abrupt end if managers do not give feedback and, as important, ask for it in return. As suggested above, training seminars are only the opening of the book. It is the manager's everyday practices and role modeling that determine what the last chapter and bottom line will say.

In my view, developmental coaching is the single most important thing a sales manager can do to increase the productivity of his or her people and to meet or exceed a business plan. Assuming the right corporate strategy, products, recruitment, and rewards, developmental coaching virtually ensures improvement in business performance and relationships. This is something the competition cannot copy. As mentioned earlier, good coaching is in the control of the sales manager (coach) and no one else. For this reason, developmental coaching is a virtual "secret weapon."

Before we look at how to give feedback and the levels of coaching, let's differentiate two kinds of feedback:

- Evaluative feedback

- Developmental feedback

Although these two kinds of feedback are interrelated, they are not different shades of the same color. They are not merely two dialects: although they are linked, look at them almost as two different languages. Understanding this is a breakthrough in shifting from boss to coach.

Evaluative Feedback

Evaluative feedback is what most people think of when they hear the word feedback. Evaluative feedback, often in the form of the annual performance review, is a key element of sales management. It is based on a familiar model of grading found in schools: A through F, a quartile, a ranking of 1 to 5. It allows for comparisons—"You outperformed/underperformed"—and it is usually related to compensation. Also, it represents yesterday, not today.

Evaluative feedback is an essential part of management. Evaluative feedback comprises the bulk of the feedback given during an annual performance review or performance assessment. During the performance review, the manager gives (and should give) a grade or rating—a *snapshot or picture of the past*—that captures the manager's perception of the person being evaluated. Some organizations include other evaluations to create what they call 360-degree feedback in which the person gets feedback from people over, under, and next to him or her as well as for clients. Some organizations even talk about "540-degree" feedback that provides clients' views. While this may stretch the bounds of geometry, it makes a point. Feedback should come from all around—and beyond.

The primary goal of the performance review where evaluative feedback is given is to make sure the person being evaluated clearly understands (not necessarily agrees with) what the grade/rating/picture is for the past. Whether evaluative feedback comes from one person or many, it is a vital part of management. (Please see Chapter 7 for performance reviews.)

Developmental Feedback

Developmental feedback is very different from evaluative feedback. It looks forward to what "we" (coach and person being coached) can do to improve and create a better picture (grade) for the future/next time. If an Olympic athlete gets an 8.8, it does not make him or her better or worse. It is a score, a grade, an evaluation. Only what happens before and after that score can make the star better or worse.

Developmental feedback answers the questions, "What can we do better to meet/exceed the plan?" or "How can we fix...?" Another key difference is that these developmental questions are not asked only once or twice a year but daily. *The time for developmental coaching is always—in a coaching session, in the corridor.*

When one manager learned the difference between evaluation and developmental feedback, he was greatly relieved. He said, "That's great. You mean I don't have to evaluate my people every time I meet with one of them?"

Development happens with developmental coaching. Moreover, *empowerment* happens with developmental coaching, not evaluative. Developmental feedback empowers because it helps people identify the obstacles they face and reinforces *their* role in removing the obstacles each day. Developmental coaching helps people live and thrive in the Stretch Zone. For a comparison of evaluative and developmental feedback, see Figure 1-1.

Evaluative Feedback	Developmental Feedback
Presents a picture of what has happened in the *past*.	Aims to improve *future* performance.
Assigns a grade—A, B, C, D—or a number—1, 2, 3, 4, 5—to past performance. Often associated with compensation.	Gives information about the impact of a salesperson's behavior to help him/her to be more successful in the future.
Is usually given quarterly or annually.	Is given 365 days a year.
Is more often formalized and paperwork-driven.	Is not usually formalized or paperwork-driven.
Is more one-way.	Is participative.
Focuses on the individual.	Focuses on the collective "we"—"what we can do."

Figure 1-1   Feedback at a glance.

The Balance

Both evaluative and developmental feedback are essential to development. In an evaluative session, 90 percent of the feedback should be evaluative, and in a developmental coaching session, 90 percent plus of the feedback should be developmental. The evaluative session and the developmental session are different and it is important to separate them. A developmental coaching session is not the time for evaluation. And an evaluative coaching session is not the time for developmental coaching. But the two are clearly linked. The evaluation (grades) should be used as a platform for development: The grade is X and the action plan is Y. The grade is the evaluative piece, and the action plan is the developmental one.

Formal evaluative coaching should take place one to four times a year. At the quarterly or annual performance review, it is "game time." Practices are over. Having developed "players" all week, the coach now chooses who will play. Quarterly reviews are a way to help red-flag performance problems and to recognize superior performance. But even in a performance review session the focus should not be solely on the past. The coach also needs to plan for the present and future.

Performance review feedback can be emotionally charged, since it often is tied to pay and involves assessment. People often get disappointed or upset during a "negative" performance review and relieved or elated during a "positive" one. Neither range of emotions is helpful to a developmental session. Since evaluative feedback can overwhelm the developmental part, it is better to *separate* the two kinds of feedback into different sessions. However, if the person is open to it, the evaluative feedback session can end with a bridge to a developmental session right there and then or, if not, with a plan for a developmental meeting a few days later.

Without *ongoing* developmental coaching, performance reviews are traumatic—filled with surprises, disagreements, and/or bad feelings. Developmental feedback can change this. Because it is ongoing, the developmental approach takes the sting, anguish, aggravation, and, most important, the surprise from performance evaluation by making it a *summary* of what has been communicated all along. Most important, developmental coaching sessions make the evaluative feedback more positive.

Shifting from boss to coach begins with a sales manager examining his or her own attitudes about feedback. Does the sales manager worry about getting feedback or does he or she seek it out? Is the feedback he or she gives only judgmental (to give a grade) or also developmental (to help improve)? What is his or her intent—to help or to coach? Does he or she view feedback as a problem or a gift?

When a manager's attitude about feedback is negative, he or she will communicate this. Unless the manager is coming from the right place and is open to feedback personally, he or she cannot help others become receptive. The sales manager first and foremost is a role model. People watch more than they listen, and the message the manager sends is the true teacher.

Two Models

The "Boss" Model—Coaching by Telling

Managers manage pretty much the way they themselves were managed. The predominant form of managing is the boss-as-expert model—"I'll tell you what to do to fix...." This assumes: (1) the manager is the one who can identify the right/priority problem or obstacle, can assess the source and magnitude of the problem or obstacle, and has the knowledge and skill to correct it; and (2) by playing the role of the expert, the manager can *best help the person being coached change and improve.* Needless to say there are significant problems with these assumptions. As for the first assumption, suppose the manager has misdiagnosed? What if the manager magnifies or minimizes the problem? What if the manager is working on the wrong problem? What if he or she lacks the expertise and know-how? The second assumption is no less flawed—is telling a person what to do the best way to help him or her improve?

Our company was working with a client in the area of sales training. When we inquired about coaching, we were told that managers had already been trained to coach. In discussing this further we learned that the company used what they called an "S-

1" model of coaching. We were told that their people—highly paid professionals in one of the most respected multinational companies in the world—had been diagnosed as *not* ready for anything other than S-1. What was S-1? It was a coaching approach in which managers told people what to do. After a brief discussion about how it was working, how people felt about it, and how people were developing, the client saw the need to change this—fast.

Most often the manager-as-expert model is not so explicit, but it is there. The manager-as-expert model is the one most people know and recall when they think of management. It is the one most people experience. Managers or experts spout out answers. The problem is that in doing so they miss a chance to help the person they are managing to grow and learn how to help himself/herself next time. All it would take to change this are four simple words: *"What do you think?"* Surely there are times for "instant coaching" and spray-paint answers, but this should not be a way of life. Too many proactive on-the-spot coaching opportunities are lost because of the ask-the-expert habit.

To understand how prevalent this model is, think about the thousands of salespeople who right now are asking their bosses questions like, "X is on the phone about....What pricing should I give him?" or "What shall I tell her?" Think about the number of bosses telling them what to do instead of asking them what they *think* they should do.

The "Coach" Model—Coaching by Asking

An alternative to the expert model is the coaching model in which a manager positions him or herself *not* as the expert but as a resource—*coach/resource versus boss/expert.* That does not mean the coach doesn't direct or add value—she or he can and should. But rather than being the source of knowledge, the coach uses knowledge and skills as *tools* to help people figure out problems and ultimately self-coach. This process helps the salesperson not only solve problems but overcome future obstacles using not only the skills, etc., but the coaching process itself. In addition to this, since few managers in today's complex environment can have *all* the answers all the time, the resource model makes more sense. It frees managers up to use the team and other resources and it helps make salespeople responsible for their own performance after training.

When there is a high performer who is so good that the manager is at a loss to know how to coach him or her, the coach can ask the person what he or she wants to work on next. The coach can also tap into others with experience by asking, "Have you talked to so and so about this?" Creating a culture where people feel comfortable reaching out to resources is absolutely essential to creative thinking, new ideas, and all-around development.

Coaching and Feedback —a Closer Look

D evelopmental coaching is a mindset and a process; it is not a set of techniques to be compared with another set of techniques. First and foremost, developmental coaching is a *philosophy* of developing people based on a commitment to their development. With the mindset in place, the process and skills are the easy part.

Developmental coaching stems from three premises about people—first, people should be involved and responsible for their own development; second, people need to be developed as well as evaluated; and third, most people want to do a good job—most people would probably not do things the wrong way if they knew a better way!

Developmental coaching is about one thing: helping the salesperson identify his or her obstacles and overcome them. A manager who can coach can guide a salesperson through the developmental "maze." Throughout this process, the coach can learn a lot about the person—how good is this salesperson at assessing the situation? What does the salesperson think the chief obstacle is? Is the salesperson capable of identifying the obstacle? What about fixing it? Does he or she have the insight, the skill? The attitude? What about effort?

The Coaching Conversation

Let's look at a few real-life "coaching" conversations to see how the manager does in terms of skill.

Conversation 1

> SALES MANAGER: Mary, you interrupted me. I was headed in X direction and you cut that discussion off. You interjected your idea and went straight into your product discussion....It was obvious the customer wanted to tell us more about....I was learning....In the future, don't jump in. You didn't see where I was going. Get to know the customer. Okay?
>
> SALESPERSON: Oh, okay. I was afraid we would run short of time, and I wanted to be sure to get to X.
>
> SALES MANAGER: Well, don't throw off the discussion if you don't know where I am going. Don't get to the product so fast.
>
> SALESPERSON: OK, but I was just concerned about time.

What did the sales manager learn about the salesperson's perceptions of the call? What was the salesperson's obstacle? What did this exchange do to correct the problem? Do we know if the person knows how to correct this kind of problem in the future? What does the manager expect? What did the manager learn? What did the salesperson learn? What will the salesperson do next time? What did this exchange do to the relationship between the two?

Conversation 2

> SALES MANAGER: Bob, I want to talk with you about your newsletter. Some of the folks in production feel you should tighten it up a little. Okay?
>
> SALESPERSON: What do you mean? I do a great job. See if they can do better. Who's complaining?
>
> SALES MANAGER: I think you do a good job. Don't worry about it. Just look it over before you send it out next time.

How much has Bob learned about what is lacking in his newsletter? How much better will the newsletter be next time? What was the obstacle?

Before we look at what's wrong, let's acknowledge what's right. These managers are, in many ways, steps ahead of many of their peers in that they are at least attempting to give feedback to their people. They are trying to be helpful and fix a perceived problem. But now let's ask what is wrong. Ask yourself, "Bossing?" "Coaching?" "Hedging?" Clearly in neither of these situations was the obstacle sought or found. This must be what the manager meant when he said, "I'm wondering if what I do when I `coach' is really coaching."

The first example is a classic example of the expert model of coaching. The manager diagnosed what was wrong and prescribed a corrective action. In the second situation, the manager's feedback was so watered down that the message was completely lost. What often passes for coaching happened at the extremes— either managers tell, tell, tell, ignore, ignore, ignore, or avoid, avoid, avoid. Extremes are always easy. Many managers go for days or months without giving *any* feedback. Some wait until the situation is at a crisis stage or they are literally ready to explode.

Being a good coach is not easy. Coaching effectively is simple, but doing it is not easy! Most second graders get more helpful feedback (gold stars/report cards) than the average salesperson!

The real problem with both of these coaching examples is that a piece of information is missing. Technically, feedback was given in these two situations, but the feedback did not lead to greater understanding or correction. Why not? Although there are several reasons, the most significant is that there was no self-assessment by the salesperson. The coach did (or tried to do) the assessing and directing. What was clearly missing was the salesperson's side of the picture. What was Mary and Bob's assessment? Why?

What did they think or feel they could do about it? The golden rule of feedback—"They talk first"—was missing.

Feedback—The Rules

Let's look at 17 guiding rules for giving developmental feedback and then look at the coaching process.

"They Talk First"

These are the golden words of developmental coaching. By *asking* the salesperson to self-assess, *before giving the coach's own view,* the coach not only gains insight into the salesperson's judgment and knowledge but also can put the responsibility for development on the salesperson.

Another reason the salesperson goes first is that it gives the coach a chance to find common ground and make other points with comments like, "Yes, that's it," or, "You forgot to mention..." or, "I meant to emphasize...."

Balancing Feedback—Positives and Areas for Improvement

Start with positives (strengths)—even if people say they only want to hear the negatives. Why begin with strengths? Not just to be nice, although that does not hurt, but because people learn as much (or more) from positive feedback as from negative. Without hearing positives, people might misinterpret the negative feedback and think it is your total feeling about them. You must make it clear it is not. When you give the positives, don't handle them like throwaways. Give as much energy to them as you do to telling the negatives. The positives must be genuine. This ties to a coach's belief that his or her people are good.

One national sales manager described the one and only time she got feedback in the past *three* years. She hated it. The reason—her manager gave her one positive piece of feedback, which she described as "throwing her a bone," before his tirade of negatives.

She was not alone. One man—who approached me at the end of a negotiation speech I had given to about 200 people—explained why he hadn't raised his hand when I asked for two volunteers for a role play. He described a terrible experience several years earlier when he had volunteered to be the salesperson in a role play in front of a group of about 100 people. He said, "That speaker tore me to shreds. When he gave me his book at the end of his speech, I threw it on the table. He had humiliated me!"

This salesperson then went on to tell how much he appreciated the balance of positive and negative feedback I had given to the role play volunteers in our audience. He said, "It was constructive. It didn't come off as criticism. We learned about our problems—but it was in a helpful, balanced way."

Although I had in fact given direct and honest negative feedback, I believe it was well received for several reasons: First and foremost I gave the positive feedback first, before "areas for improvement." I did not refer to them as "negatives." I did tone down the areas for improvement *slightly,* since this was not a one-on-one situation but a large group forum in which one person had been singled out. I also helped prepare people to *value* feedback as a way to *get to the next level.* I stressed that no one can progress in work or life just doing what he or she is currently doing. Finally, I approached the volunteer who was to get the feedback as "everyman," representing all of us.

Increase the Amount of Positive Feedback Up Front

Most coaches need to increase the amount of positive feedback they give up front. By doing so they can start out a coaching session by sending the message that they feel the salesperson is competent, or at least is doing some things right. This builds a positive foundation that makes it easier for the person receiving the feedback to accept the areas for improvement. But the heart of this is the feeling that the person is good or has the potential to be good. This in turn forms a foundation for *trust.*

Without trust, the developmental coaching process doesn't really work. Fortunately, the process of coaching can help create and build trust and avoid misunderstandings and distrust.

It is a bit like the chicken-and-egg debate. It is not a matter of which comes first. Trust and skill go hand in hand. Experience shows that a coach who has a positive attitude about his or her people and has coaching skills can have tremendous impact.

By using positives as well as areas for improvement, the coach can not only build trust but can keep things in perspective. The truth is that no one is 100 percent effective or 100 percent ineffective. Therefore, it is up to the person giving feedback to be able to observe *both* the strengths and areas for improvement.

When unsure of how much to give of each, coaches should err on the side of positives. It is also important to realize that many salespeople want to focus on the negatives, and they need help to *hear* the positives and not dismiss them.

If a coach really can't find any positives, it is important *not* to make them up. The basic rule is to be honest. In such a situation the coach might say, "Because I am so focused on X, I'm not really seeing positives" or "I'm trying to look for positives and am coming up short!" Whenever possible, however, the coach should acknowledge the positives to put things in perspective and to establish common ground. When the coach disagrees with the positives the salesperson identifies, he or she should ask for specifics around them. When the coach agrees with the positives, he or she can build on them.

Here are some examples of balancing strengths and areas for improvement when giving feedback:

- "Beth, I know you are putting in long days and handling 'fires' around here everyday. Believe me, I am well aware of that and appreciate the job you are doing. Today I want to talk with you about your prospecting effort. I have looked at your call reports, and I noticed that of the 12 calls you planned to make over the past week, three were with prospective clients. Our priority and focus at this time is *new* business. How does your effort support that?" or "Why three prospect calls?" (Get salesperson's perception.)

- "Look, Joe, I know you were here long into the night on Thursday to finish the proposal. In spite of that there seems to be problems. Tom called me to say there were several errors in the proposal that he feels cost us the deal. What happened?"

- "Mike, I'd like to give my perceptions. I agree that you were excellent in summarizing the client's objectives and in describing our response to those objectives. In addition to that, I really liked…(coach's positives). And you were great on getting clarification on….I think a key area for you to work on is your description of our firm. You emphasized our capabilities in….While generally that is fine, did any of that relate to *this* client? Since they do…, there was a chance to link to the client's interest. What could you have said to tie to that? What do you think? (Check perceptions.) In your followup what will you emphasize about us for them?"

Of course, there will also be times when a problem is so severe that it warrants discussion without anything else on the agenda. The point is that there should be many, many more times when more balanced feedback is given. In situations when the coach can't find an area for improvement, for example, with a "top performer," the coach can ask him or her to identify an area to work on next. Together they can figure out resources to support this development.

While some coaches don't give positives, many are uncomfortable giving feedback on the negatives. This usually results in giving no feedback at all. By understanding that it is appropriate and *preferable* to give *both* strengths and areas for improvement, many coaches can get more comfortable with feedback. What they formerly saw as "bad news" they now begin to see as a part of a total development process to help their people see and achieve possibilities.

Have Courage

People deserve feedback. They have the right to try to fix things. They can't do that if they are not aware of what to fix. Coaches need the courage to say the "hard" things. Managers have the obligation to give feedback. One manager recognized this when he said, "I'd be pretty angry if my boss withheld information from me that could ultimately hurt my career." Managers need to believe in and know how to give specific, balanced feedback. You can give feedback on any business topic the salesperson can correct.

Remember, as you talk about areas for improvement, *describe them as such, not as negatives.* "Areas for improvement" matches the concept of getting to the next level of excellence and the level after that.

Be Specific

As you prepare to coach and give feedback, take the time to line up specific examples so the person getting the feedback can understand your message. Find current examples; don't rely on "ancient history." Avoid giving general feedback, for example, don't say, "You have a bad attitude" and stop there. Focus on specific behaviors—actions, inactions, words, tones, body signals, facial expressions, etc.—that in your mind manifest "bad attitude" and discuss these instead. Describe when, where, and how often you have seen these behaviors.

One manager would have been on shaky ground had he said, "You need to change your attitude" and left it at that. Instead he gave feedback on the salesperson's behaviors in *concrete detail:* consistently arriving late for weekly sales meetings, choosing a seat outside the group, failing to contribute, keeping her head down throughout the meeting, and grimacing as certain topics were discussed. The salesperson acknowledged the behaviors, and at least the problem was out on the table. The manager then asked her for her view of the impact of her behaviors on her teammates and herself, and the coaching dialogue began.

The more specific the feedback, the better. We saw this many years ago with one of our new trainers. No matter how much training, coaching, and observation time we gave to her, she could not catch on to the most basic parts of our core program. Worse yet, she did not realize she was not catching on! After months of coaching and feedback, her manager and I met with her and asked her how she felt she was doing. "Great!" she replied. "I'm really coming along. I know all the modules and I'm ready." When we told her our impression and shared feedback from other trainers who felt uncomfortable teaming with her, she strongly disagreed. She was adamant to the point of being abrasive. She *could* do the job and *would* do the job, and that was that. Her manager then walked out of the conference room and returned, carrying the flip chart he had used with her in her most recent train-the-trainer session. He flipped through several pages—"This is what you covered, but this is what was supposed to be covered..." and so on and so on for 5 pages. A look of utter surprise appeared on her face. In one day she resigned. It wasn't until she was given absolute, concrete examples—pages of them—that she was able to see the mismatch. Of course, the purpose of feedback is to help people grow, *correct* problems, and *succeed,* but it also can help individuals realize when it is time to cut their losses.

Focus on a Few Key Things—
Don't Overload

No one can work on 20 things at once. If you don't limit your feedback, you will overwhelm and overload the receiver. Everyone has a saturation point: people can absorb and work on just so much. Therefore, developmental feedback is incremental. That is the beauty of it. Focusing on one point at a time also allows for what we in our company call "short hand" coaching in which we can coach during the action in about two minutes.

Also, for a coaching session as you prepare to give feedback, particularly at first, limit the areas for improvement to one or two key points per session, at most, so that the person can work on those before tackling the next obstacle. Even if you feel there are numerous important problems, don't try to cover the waterfront. Figure out which problem is most pressing and work on it. Choose one or two things that will make the most difference.

Close the Door

Reserve individual, in-depth, negative feedback for one-on-one sessions. Feedback in a group setting is not appropriate for in-depth feedback directed to one person. Group feedback is appropriate only if it impacts the team and if the team is ready for group feedback. (Please see Chapter 8 for discussion on coaching the team.)

You can say almost anything to someone one-on-one. Even if you go too far or get out of line, a comment later like, "I'm sorry, I was out of line," can usually heal the harshest exchange of words—*if they were exchanged in privacy*. But if you embarrass someone in front of others—if you cause someone to lose face—you risk creating a long-term enemy and causing irreversible damage to your relationship.

Such was the case of a retired salesperson who, when hired by his former company to run a sales training seminar for a newly hired group of trainees, *abused* his feedback rights as a trainer. During a seminar that I, as a consultant, had the misfortune to witness, he humiliated one of the participants because of the participant's approach to a problem. The participant had said he would be "less than honest" with the client in the case situation. Instead of asking the participant why he felt being "less than honest" would be acceptable in this firm and then *clearly* defining the firm's ethical position and asking the young man to see him at the end of the session, this former senior salesman attacked the participant's values, ethics, and character as his associates watched and waited. The young man sat motionless as the tirade went on *and on*. The only sign of the young man's reaction was the quivering of his lower lip. Three weeks later, this hand-selected candidate (one of 60 out of 500) resigned from the program, saying he did not feel he could recover from this stigma and humiliation.

But the story did not end there. The atmosphere from this event lingered throughout the three-month training program. Fear was the name of the game. The tragedy is that this seasoned salesperson had an opportunity to influence not only that trainee but 59 other young people on the values of the firm. But instead, because of his lack of judgment, his insensitivity, and his lack of skill in how far to go with his feedback in public, he caused unnecessary harm all around. Management was upset with the salesperson's "antics" and gave this "loose cannon" to me for coaching. The amazing part is that he began to change. At first he totally rejected giving positive feedback, but once he did it he resolved to continue to do so, he told me, in the seminars and *at home.*

Everyone knows that a manager (in the case the trainer) has the authority to crack down on an offender; but restraint, especially in public, is far more powerful. A perfect example of this brand of humility was exhibited by a judge in a nationally televised trial when he apologized to a prosecutor at a crucial point early in the trial. The judge had been unflinching in his decision to hold the prosecutor in contempt if he did not apologize to the court, but the judge exceeded all expectations when after receiving the prosecutor's apology, he apologized in return.

Be Open and Honest

The ultimate goal of coaching is to have an environment that is open and honest. One of the organizations we work with refers to such sessions as "open and honest." This kind of acceptance starts with a coach who in privacy is open and honest with his/her people or colleagues. Pulling punches does not usually help anyone. The coach must have the courage to say what others might be afraid to bring up. The rule of thumb is to give feedback on anything the person can conceivably fix that relates to the work at hand. For example, if someone is short, growing taller is not a topic for coaching. By contrast, anything a person can change that relates to the task to be done is fair game. Of course, don't be brutal or judgmental, but don't water down the feedback so that the person misses the message. The role of the coach is to help his or her people succeed, and people have a right to know any information the coach has about the coach's perception of obstacles that may be hindering that success.

Be on Time

Coaching is often approached as a series of isolated incidences to correct a problem. Or it may surface in now-or-never "triage coaching," which is used when things go out of control. "Triage coaching" attempts to change things radically in a short time frame. It is highly reactive, and it is often touch-and-go. Unfortunately, it often shows up as the annual performance evaluation where in 1 hour a manager attempts to make changes that should have begun 11 months and 29 days before. The focus of a triage coaching session often is the "worst case" scenario, rather than a developmental or strategic session. It does not usually integrate or build, and there is little connection to the company's long-term plans. When it is eleventh-hour coaching, the goal is usually to get the valleys to the flat line (neutral performance), not to reach the peaks.

The goal is to give feedback often and in a timely manner, *close to the event.* When giving feedback on a specific event, unless people are upset and need time to calm down, give that feedback *as close to the time of the event as possible.* If not, problems will fester. First of all, quick feedback will be helpful in preventing the same problem from occurring again. Second, the event will be fresh, and therefore, the coaching is likely to have more impact and importance. In the long run, giving feedback "as you go" is the best approach, because it eliminates surprises at performance review time, and it prevents things from bottling up or getting out of control. Timeliness applies not only to negative feedback but to positive feedback as well. If someone successfully mollifies an angry client, the time to comment is while traveling away from the session—not a month later.

Don't Be a Go-between

Whenever possible, don't fight battles for your people when a third party is involved. This doesn't mean that a coach shouldn't support his or her people. On the contrary, support is vital. But, for example, if a salesperson complains about someone internally, the best strategy, although it often is met with resistance, is to coach the salesperson on how to give the feedback directly to that person. A typical go-between conversation goes like this:

Don't

> SALESPERSON: X (an internal colleague) gave us lousy pricing again. We lost the deal. This is the second time this week. You have to help me with Joe. What can you do?
>
> SALES MANAGER (as go-between): What happened?…I'll talk to Joe (or Joe's manager). Don't worry. I'll take care of this.

Do

> SALESPERSON: X gave us lousy pricing again. We lost the deal. This is the second time this week. You have to help me with Joe. What can you do?
>
> COACH: That doesn't sound good. What happened?…*Have you spoken to Joe?*
>
> SALESPERSON: It won't do any good. He won't listen to me. You know that.

COACH: Well, have you talked to him about this? (repeat question)

SALESPERSON: No. But it won't do any good.

COACH: Well, before we go around him, what do you think about giving him feedback directly so he understands how you feel and the impact he is having?

People at all levels in any organization often resist giving direct feedback to colleagues, especially if the culture does not support it. But as mentioned earlier, the coach's role is to help each person stretch—live in the Stretch Zone—and learn how to solve this obstacle *and the next one.*

If the person's feedback has no impact, then elevating the discussion to the managerial level may be appropriate. The salesperson's manager can speak to Joe's manager or, when there is open communication, the salesperson can talk to Joe's manager. In most organizations this does not happen because the positions and titles of the hierarchy—not the dynamics of the relationship or tasks to be accomplished—drive how things are done. A coach can change this with his or her own people by making feedback a two-way street and the norm for how they work together.

Of course, if a salesperson simply will not or cannot give feedback to the person with whom he or she is having problems, the manager can suggest a three-way conversation that includes the manager, who, in most situations, should go *with,* not *for,* him or her.

Don't Abdicate

In developmental coaching the goal is to have the salesperson learn how to identify his or her own obstacles. While this might appear to release the manager from responsibility, in fact, the primary role of the manager is to guide a person to discovery. This is a far cry from abdicating the role of coach. When asked for guidance one manager said, "Do what you think!" His people read this as disinterest. Had the manager who responded with the words, "Do what you think" inverted the words to "What do you think?" he could have coached. This question might have opened all sorts of doors to learning.

Another manager was asked by a young associate in his group for help on a project for a senior managing director. The manager replied, "I can't give you the answer." This manager was confusing coaching with telling or doing. While he had the right instinct, that indeed he should not simply "give" the "answer," he forgot to do the right thing—coach. With a few guiding questions (What do you think? Have you looked into...? Have you talked to so-and-so?), not limiting answers, the coach could have helped this salesperson develop.

Trust—and Be Trustworthy

Unless the sales manager is a good actor, he or she won't be able to fake trust and engender it in others. Salespeople in general form fairly accurate judgments about who is "for" and who is "against" them. If a coach has a positive attitude and a desire to help, he or she will get on that first "list" and—with good coaching skills—stay there.

Unless a sales manager believes his or her people are fundamentally good and capable of being even better, and unless the manager wants to be a part of their development, there isn't much hope for developmental coaching. Sales managers who succeed in developing their people for the most part believe that their people can and want to do a good job.

Great managers are good coaches, not bad cops. Their message is "I want to help," not "I'm out to get you." They reward, help, and guide, not penalize, harass, and dictate.

A person's openness to coaching is usually proportionate to

his or her level of trust. Trust is shaped by experience. Sales managers and salespeople alike have to trust themselves as well as each other.

Love Feedback

Effective coaching is a matter of know-how—knowing the coaching process and having the skills. Great *developmental* coaching is a combination of know-how and *attitude.* Again, if the coach is uncomfortable getting and/or giving feedback, he or she will undoubtedly project that discomfort. A negative attitude is contagious—and so is a positive attitude. The coach has to be truly committed to and open to giving and seeking feedback.

Give Praise

Everyone needs to feel appreciated and recognized. By taking the time to acknowledge a job well done—an effort beyond the call of duty or an important victory—a coach has a chance to create a team of excellent and empowered salespeople. Once a very talented, personable young woman in our company came and asked in an almost pleading manner for more positive feedback. We didn't get around to it very often. Within six months she resigned, and we learned a hard lesson. Her departure was a loss to us. Her performance was excellent, and she was a pleasure to work with. She always took the initiative in asking for what she needed in order to do her best work—as evidenced by her request. Most people won't come out and ask for praise as she did. Most people are resigned to not being appreciated, to feeling as if no one really cares, and to be treated like a cog in a wheel. Great companies and coaches take the time to recognize good work and good people and *encourage their people to ask for recognition when it is not forthcoming.*

Take Your Anger Temperature

The giver of feedback has to do everything he or she can to deliver the message so the recipient gets it. The more confrontational or attacking the manner, the less likely the person will be open to receiving feedback because panic or resentment will set in. This does *not* mean being dishonest or indirect. However, if the coach is very angry, then *that* will be the predominant communication, not the issue itself.

Certainly the coach has the right and the obligation as a part of being open and honest to say he or she is angry, but if he or she is "steaming," then that is *not* the time to give feedback. The anger will block the coach from listening or problemsolving and prevent the receiver of the feedback from hearing or growing. Instead, the coach can and should say, "I'm angry (frustrated/ annoyed) about..." and then set a time to get into it a little later when the smoke clears. When the coach does give the message, he or she can be direct and clear about the magnitude of the situation, but in a way that fosters results and change.

The "Feedback Conversation"

Since most people are not used to feedback, a coach would be wise to have a "feedback talk" to prepare people for developmental coaching. The coach should discuss *why* and *how* he or she will be giving feedback. Most important, the coach should say he or she wants and needs feedback back!

Be the Model

You are the role model. During coaching sessions and day to day, it is important for you to be *open to receiving* feedback as well as to giving it. Be open and honest. Say the hard things that others won't say. By your own example you can teach people how to give and take feedback.

Receiving Feedback

The person receiving feedback has a responsibility to remain open. Think about the salesperson who produced the newsletter and reacted defensively to the feedback and was able to intimidate his manager. His tactic worked in the short run—he also continued to write poor newsletters.

Since most people react defensively at first when they get "critical" feedback/areas for improvement, it can be very helpful to give people guidelines for accepting feedback:

- Recognize that your tendency will probably be to listen for what you disagree with, not what you can learn.
- Be quiet and listen with an ear to what you can learn.
- Remain quiet and don't interrupt or explain.
- Make a real effort to keep your mind on "receive," not send.
- Fight the "self talk" that tells you to reject the feedback with spoken or unspoken comments like, "He doesn't understand." "My reason for doing…was.…"
- Listen for what you can use, not what you don't agree with.
- Ask questions to learn more.
- Take notes and review the comments.
- Ask for feedback.
- Thank the giver.

Coaches need to share these guidelines with their salespeople and need to practice them when they themselves get feedback.

Level 1—the Process of Coaching

The transition from boss to coach starts with the sales manager knowing and understanding the process of developmental coaching. There are three levels of mastery in developmental sales coaching. Coaching is not something that can be mastered or accomplished overnight. It takes work to get good at it. The three levels are much like the levels of a language, for example French 101, 201, and 301. The student gains greater skill at the same basic process. The first level is to *become aware* of the process. The second level is to *get good* at it—go deep. The third level is to *use* it to really build the relationship and partnership. We will begin by looking in depth at the manager-to-salesperson coaching at the three levels.

The three levels of developmental sales coaching are:

1. Level 1—*the process.* Understanding the fundamental "process" of coaching—how to coach.

2. Level 2—*the art.* Coaching for depth—uncovering the obstacles while dealing with objections—helping people go deeper to identify and remove their obstacles.

3. Level 3—*the heart.* Building the relationship and forming the partnership between coach and salesperson.

There are no scripts or formulas for any of these levels. There is nothing rote about developmental coaching. It takes skill, focus, and commitment.

Level 1 of Developmental Coaching

Let's begin with level 1, the process. This is the foundation level. Just as there are special ways to pick up something if you have hurt your back, so there are "mechanics" unique to developmental coaching. Level 1 is the mechanics.

There are six elements to the developmental coaching process:

- **Preparing for the developmental coaching session**
- **The opening**
- **Perceptions and needs (salesperson's and coach's—in that order)**
- **Identifying and removing the obstacles**
- **Closing with an action step**
- **Follow-up**

As we go through the process it will seem like common sense. With my nearly two decades of experience, though, I feel safe in saying that it is *not* common practice.

Let's see how to make effective developmental coaching an everyday occurrence for you, your people, and your organization. While we will begin with the process for a full coaching session, the goal is to make coaching something that happens not only in formal coaching session but every day in the corridor and during the action.

Preparing for the Developmental Coaching Session

Preparation doesn't require big blocks of time, but it does require lining up four things: (1) *the primary objective*—what the coach hopes to see as a result of the meeting, (2) *specific positive feedback* the coach will give, (3) *specific areas for improvement,* and (4) *anticipation of the salesperson's reaction.* Preparation for a coaching session is often a matter of a few minutes and for on-the-spot coaching that takes place during the action—it can take less than a minute.

Setting the objective is important. A coach who doesn't know what he or she would like to see as the outcome of a coaching session is far less likely to get there than one who has a clear objective going in. Unfortunately, when coaches have an objective in mind, it is often in the form of what they do not want to see rather than a clear picture of what they expect. Positive objectives that spell out, "I'd like to see..." are certainly more helpful than those that specify what not to do.

For example, one sales manager was caught unaware during a "team" call about a serious client problem. His idea of coaching was to tell the junior salesperson, "Make sure I'm not caught short again, OK?" He told the salesperson what *not* to do, but the salesperson left with no indication of what to do. The manager might have said, "Why did this happen?" and, better yet, "What *can we do* in the future so this doesn't happen again?" The salesperson and the coach might have worked together to generate ideas about what would help—for example, a written agenda for the call a few days in advance, or a precall dialogue about the call objectives, problems, opportunities, and sensitivities in the overall relationship.

Of course, the coach's objective is only one part of the picture.

The coach still must get the salesperson's view of the situation and his or her ideas on improving the situation. The coach's objective is a starting point.

As a coach creates the objective for the session, he or she should make sure it is specific and that he or she has a clear sense of the time frame and accountability around the objective.

THE OPENING

The opening establishes two very important things: rapport and purpose.

Build Rapport

During the opening, it is important not to forget the human side. Sometimes because coaches feel that since they will be delivering "bad" news—a client complaint, a lost sale, a botched sales call, disappointing numbers, etc.—they go directly to it in an attempt to avoid "beating around the bush." But feedback—even if the main focus is "bad" news—is an interaction. Therefore, the coach should take a moment to say hello and to ask how the person is. This sets the right tone for working together. What many managers don't realize is that being "hard" on issues does not require being hard on people. As a matter of fact, the goal should be to be *easy* on people but hard on issues and measurement. Whether it is "spot" coaching (a moment on the fly) or a more formal coaching "session," it is important to spend a moment on the human side.

State the Purpose

But it is also important not to "beat around the bush." *During the opening it is very helpful to be clear and frank about the purpose of the session—without being judgmental.* The coaching session is not a "magical mystery tour." The coach should clearly state the specific goal of the meeting. This will help alleviate apprehensiveness and set a focus for the discussion.

The trap in stating the purpose is that the coach might go too far—all the way to evaluation and conclusion. For example, the coach who begins, "We have a real problem here. You're not making your new business numbers. You don't even seem to be trying. If this doesn't turn around....How many calls do you make a day anyway?,", goes too far if development, not evaluation, is his or her purpose. Any sensible person hearing that would know that the discussion, for all intents and purposes, is really over and that the most likely response would be to become defensive (and resentful).

Another example of being judgmental would be the manager who opens by saying, "I am very upset about that call. You didn't know...." While this manager is clear and direct in his or her view, he or she has left little to discuss.

A much better approach would be to state the purpose without formulating a conclusion or judgment. For example, "I want to talk about your goals for new business, since our reports indicate that your numbers are down," or, "I would like to discuss the call, in particular...." Here the statements are very clear but not evaluative. They also create a platform on which to *ask* the salesperson to assess his or her performance and the situation, rather than have the coach assess it for him or her.

Remember, while the purpose of the session should be stated directly and clearly at the outset, the *opening is not the close.* The goal is to put the topic *on* the table and begin an open dialogue. Early judgments will close down open discussion. Although the coach should be open and honest, he or she should state the purpose of the meeting without giving his or her assessment of the situation—not yet! The next element is to get the perceptions of the person being coached. Where the salesperson was not meeting his or her new business numbers, the coach would ask, "What is going on?"

COMMUNICATING PERCEPTIONS AND NEEDS

After the opening, the goal is to get the salesperson's perceptions of the situation. This rarely happens. One coach was concerned that a bright, young salesperson was spinning his wheels with prospects that did not qualify. This salesperson was spending a lot of time working on one deal but spending time with the external consultant—clearly this was a long shot in the coach's view. The coach's objective for the coaching session was to help the salespeople be more strategic in determining where to invest energy and resources. He wanted the salesperson to create a list of qualifying questions and develop a strategy to get to the economic decision maker.

Unfortunately, the "coach" began the coaching session by telling the salesperson that he didn't want the salesperson to dedicate any more time or resources to this particular prospect. The salesperson became defensive, and the session ended in angry silence.

If the coach asked questions about the salesperson's assessment of the opportunity, he could have learned that even with a consultant in the picture, the salesperson actually had a good shot at an important piece of business. A few more questions would have provided a great platform for the coach to discuss the value of getting to the economic buyer, too. And more important, the coach could have unearthed this salesperson's fear of trying to get to the senior decision maker.

The coach, going into the meeting, had strong, helpful objectives. Unfortunately, he only had half the story—his. And at the conclusion of the 15-minute session, that was still all he had.

First the Salesperson, Then the Coach

Simply put—*they talk first!* This golden rule of coaching is simple to understand and very difficult to carry out! As mentioned earlier, it is essential to get the person being coached to give his or her perception before the coach gives his or her own assessment. It is important for the coach to refrain from giving his or her view in any way at all—not even making a general comment like, "That was good." This simple principle actually helps shorten the coaching session because it helps get to the obstacle and feelings about the obstacle more quickly.

The coach's goal is to get the salesperson to self-assess one or more specific areas. There are three core questions for coaches to ask so that people talk first:

1. "How do you see the situation?"
   ("How do you think that went?" "What's going on?" "What happened with...?" "How is...coming along?" "Why?" "What do you want to work on?")

In the past year I have noticed that more and more managers are actually beginning coaching sessions with these questions (roughly about 30 percent). The problem is salespeople usually respond very briefly and in general terms. Managers then quickly take over and go into a telling mode.

The fact is salespeople often give limited answers, and if the coach does not ask at least two more questions, he or she won't get a real coaching dialogue.

2. "What did you do well?" "What are the positives?" "Be specific."

3. "What is an area for improvement?" "What could you (we) have done better?" "Be specific."

This is the essence of coaching by asking versus coaching by telling. By asking these three basic questions (or variations of them) the coach can foster self-assessment that can lead to growth and commitment.

For example, the coach might open by saying, "I want to talk about your goals for new business, since our reports indicate that your numbers are down" (Purpose), and then ask, "What is happening with your new business efforts?" This approach provides an opportunity for the person being coached to think, to self-assess, and to maintain his or her integrity. It pushes the person to identify the obstacles and take responsibility for development.

Once the person being coached has given his or her perception of what is going on, where things stand, what happened, and why—then the coach can give his or her own perceptions. The typical "manager," however, does one of two things after opening: (1) directly comes out and *tells* the person what he or she thinks is wrong and right or (2) asks for the person's perception, but merely *as a quick formality.* After getting a general short answer from the salesperson ("Great, I think we'll get the business" or "Not good. I couldn't get through"), within a few seconds the manager is *telling* the salesperson all about his or her own assessment of the situation.

Although the coach must be prepared, he or she should guard against falling into the trap of the expert model in which he or she comes to the session sure of the obstacle and ready to fix it. If the coach has identified the wrong obstacle, he or she then creates a new problem on top of the existing one. In addition to this, not giving the salesperson a chance to have input early can slight his or her integrity. Moreover, the coach gets no insight into what the salesperson understands or does not understand.

Salespeople themselves are perpetuators of the "expert" model. Accustomed to being told what to do, they look to their managers for answers. They encourage managers to put on their "expert" cap and tell them what was good or bad, and what to do about it.

Because most salespeople don't get asked to self-assess, when they are asked they can be suspicious. Some look at it as a set up. They may try to avoid taking ownership with comments like, "You're the boss; tell me what to do!" or "You know what you want; so just tell me." Unless the manager is grounded in the value of coaching and knows how to coach, he or she will probably comply. But a coach who understands that people need to know how to self-assess if they are to develop will put the responsibility where it belongs—on the salesperson.

Managers get opportunities to coach this every day. When a salesperson says, "How did I do?," or even more commonly, "What should I do about...?," the coach can decide not to jump in with an answer. Instead he or she can ask, "How do *you* think you did?" or "I have some ideas I'd like to discuss, but *first* I'd like to hear what *you* think you should do?" or "What do you think?" If the salesperson resists or holds back, a coach persists in encouraging the salesperson to self-assess. With this on the table the coach can give his or her perceptions—"I agree with...I'd also like to tell you how I saw...." Everyone has blind spots and the coach's view is needed, *but only after the salesperson's*!

One manager who failed to ask these questions upset a good relationship with his top sales producer. The salesperson had quoted the client a price of $85,000 for a multiple-product package. The manager, assuming the package included three items that were commonly grouped together, was furious that his salesperson would set such low pricing. When the salesperson came into the office, the manager attacked him, "Who gave you the authority to give our services away? How could you sell A, B, and C for $85,000? What were you thinking? Don't think this won't affect your commission!" In fact, as the manager soon learned, his assumptions were entirely wrong. The salesperson had sold the client only the *first part* of the package for $85,000.

Had the manager asked, "Gary, X says he's paying $85,000. How did you price it?" or "What's he getting?" or "What's that all about?" he could have avoided a strain on a relationship. Then, *if* there was a problem, he could have gone deeper—"What did you base that pricing on?" "Why?" "What is your understanding of how we price?" With this approach, developmental coaching could have started! Instead, assumptions led to recriminations and hard feelings. It bears repeating: Developmental coaching is hard on issues and soft on people.

This is easier said than done. Almost everyone intellectually accepts the concept of "They talk first." But living it is another thing altogether. The concept "They talk first" makes the critical difference between coaching and bossing. It is the beginning of moving from the expert model to the resource model. It is the beginning of empowerment in its most practical and powerful form.

The halo benefit—beyond improving performance—is that people working with the coach become increasingly independent. As one company says in its mission statement, "The good manager is the manager who is not missed when he or she leaves." What this means is that he or she has developed his or her people so that they are independent. One coach puts it this way, "My job is to make my people better than I am."

The Coach Reinforces Common Ground and Gives His or Her Perceptions

A good coach is a good listener. Once the salesperson self-assesses, the coach can comment on the areas where the two of them see eye-to-eye. It is the coach's job to listen for and hopefully find these areas. For example, two colleagues in a *Fortune* 100 company, one a regional generalist and one the technical specialist from headquarters, met with their client. After the meeting, the specialist began to summarize next steps. The generalist interrupted and in a hostile tone said, "I'm the *local* contact. I'm the one the client has to call and work with daily. You undermined me. You monopolized the meeting...." The technical specialist responded defensively—"Well I know the...products...." The confrontation ended in a stalemate with two "teammates" walking out in a huff. The result: bad feelings and no client plan. All their energy got invested in internal competition, rather than the client. With some coaching skills the situation could have had a better ending.

In fact, these peers had identical goals. The specialist had no desire to be the day-to-day contact. The generalist did not want to be the technical specialist. But they were incapable of peer coaching. Ideally, one of them could have created common ground. What if the specialist said, "I agree that you are the local contact and the client does work with you day to day" (showing empathy, acknowledging). "I feel concerned that you feel I monopolized the show. Why?...What role do you feel I should play?" (questioning, getting input). If there really were points of agreement, the specialist might have said, "I hear what you are saying. I still don't understand why...I have to let you know my view is different...." (For more information on peer coaching, please see Chapter 9.)

Give Your Perceptions as Coach

After the salesperson gives feedback on his or her own performance, the coach can give his or her perceptions of strengths and areas for improvement. When it is the coach's turn to talk, words like "This is my perception...Here's why...," or, "Here's what I think..." have great impact, especially when the coach has specific examples of strengths first and areas for improvement. It is important that the coach do this after he or she hears the salesperson's perception. Although a coach probably will have a "best guess" based on the experience, knowledge, and attitudes of the coach about the salesperson's obstacle, at best that guess reflects only a *partial* picture—the coach's view. Key data are missing: the view of the person being coached. (Please see discussion of feedback in Chapter 2.)

IDENTIFYING AND REMOVING THE OBSTACLES

The good coach takes a focused approach to obstacles—first checking, then looking more deeply, and, finally, helping the salesperson remove the obstacle.

Before anything can be fixed there must be some acknowledgment that there is a problem. When there is a fundamental difference in perceptions, the coach should use questions to get at this. And then the coach can reiterate his or her specific feedback, citing examples again. Of course, when this does not meet with success, the coach can pull rank and restate standards, objectives, and vision, and demand a certain behavior change. There is certainly a time and place for what one coach called his "the train has left the station and it is going one direction—either you are on or off" speech. However, most of the time there can be a meeting of the minds about the obstacle. Without it, the coach is likely to get minimal effort—compliance at best or sabotage at worst. Since most people ultimately will do what they want to anyway, it makes a lot of sense to try to get the buy-in of people, and a simple way to do this is to get and respect their input.

Removing the Obstacle and Letting the Salesperson Suggest the Solution

Once the key obstacle is on the table and understood, the work of removing the obstacle can begin. This is another place where the "coach" may be tempted to "boss." The process of removing obstacles includes:

• Asking the salesperson to describe the desired outcome.

• Asking the salesperson to generate options.

• Asking the salesperson to suggest the output of the coaching session or next step.

Once a problem is identified, most managers *tell* the salesperson what to do. Of course, marching orders might solve the immediate problem, but not the next one. It can be very eye-opening for the coach to ask the person being coached to suggest an idea, next step, or game plan.

Here is an example of a revealing coaching session—10 minutes into a discussion about an irate client's complaint about poor follow-up:

COACH: What do you think you should do at this point?

SALESPERSON: I'll call her first thing Monday morning. (*It was Friday.*)

COACH: (*Thinking "Monday! What about* now*?"*) Monday? Why Monday?...How much of a priority is this?

Using the "boss" mode, a sales manager probably would have instructed, "Call the client now." The client's problem may have been solved then and there, but the salesperson's problem with a sense of urgency, setting priorities, and follow-up would probably have lived on and on.

Developmental coaching enables the coach to understand where the salesperson is. The goal of coaching is to help the person being coached understand what his or her obstacles are and overcome them. Once the obstacle is identified, a question like, "Well, what do you think you (we) should do?" can open doors to progress. As the coach assesses the person's plan, he or she should distinguish the "what" from the "how." As one coach phrased it, *"What* we are going to do is set in stone. There is room in *how* we will do it."

The good news is that salespeople's solutions can exceed the expectations of their coaches. For example, when one salesperson was asked what he could do in the future not to miss a cross-sell opportunity with an 800 call-in customer, he did not simply make a commitment for the future but asked his coach to listen in while he redialed the customer with whom he had missed an opportunity. That call ended with the sale of two additional products and a thank you from the customer. Of course, if the solution the salesperson suggests is not satisfactory, the coach can help reshape it.

If the person being coached cannot come up with a solution, the coach should push by asking the person to focus on what he or she can do that is in his or her immediate control. Coaches often assume too much responsibility, frequently delegating things to *themselves.* The goal is to put the accountability on the salesperson. When the person really cannot come up with an idea, the coach can offer one as an option or idea, not an answer. But it is vital that the coach use this as a jumping point, asking the person how he or she feels about the solution and, more important, *why.*

Sometimes when salespeople do offer a solution they suggest one that is outside their own control. For example, they may suggest being sent to a training seminar, getting an administrative assistant, or having the manager take the responsibility—for example, make the call. Do not take the bait! Of course, these ideas may have merit and may be possible, but it is essential to bring the issue back to the individual salesperson. By all means acknowledge and consider those ideas, but always ask, "What can *you* do *now* that is in *your control?*"

Of course, it may make perfect sense for a person to suggest "going to a sales seminar" or "seeing you (the coach) do X," but it is also important that the person identifies something he or she can do differently.

One of the outputs of good coaching is the person being coached becomes more internal ("I am a factor in what happens to me") versus external ("I am a victim"—whining and blaming everything else). Successful people in all walks of life, not only in sales, are "internal." They attribute their success in great part to what *they* do. They believe they make things happen. They live in the Stretch Zone. "External" people, on the other hand, believe things *happen* to them. They attribute their lot in life to things such as "being in the right place," "who you know," "luck," "being 'X,' not 'Y,'" etc.

Once an idea of what to do is on the table, the coach can practice and demonstrate to support what can follow. For example, the coach might role-play a situation, brainstorm a list of questions, review a strategy, and offer other kinds of support.

For example, one salesperson was far behind his peers in "closing" business. As his coach described it, they used what he called a "soft sell" because his salespeople technically did not close. Their close was to influence whether their clients purchased their product over the competition's at a later date—much the way a pharmaceutical sales rep "sells" to a physician who will later write or not write a prescription, using the rep's product. In the coaching session, the coach and the rep devised a close for this "soft" kind of sell. After working on it for about 10 minutes they created this close: "Given what we talked about, next time you are in the market, will you give us an even shot? Will you...?" This close, along with a few other skill improvements, helped one salesperson improve his results—and literally saved his job.

CLOSE WITH AN ACTION STEP

Developmental coaching is about incremental growth, taking small steps to make big gains. The key is to end the coaching session with ideally one, maybe two, specific, agreed-upon *action steps* that the person being coached will take. Setting a specific *time frame to follow up* is also essential. Unless the action step is measurable or observable and the time to accomplish it is set, it will be very difficult to monitor. Once the action step is set, the coach should ask the salesperson to summarize. For example, "For the next call I will prepare strategic questions and then focus on questioning early in the call." Then once questioning is "conquered," the next area for growth can be explored.

The final part of the close is the place for the coach to be the cheerleader by wrapping up with words of encouragement. A phrase—when genuine—like, "I know you can do it," can mean a lot. And when appropriate—which should be often—the coach should ask for feedback.

FOLLOW-UP

People read follow-up or a lack of follow-up as the true sign of what does or does not really matter. Follow-up not only helps maintain momentum and creates an atmosphere of accountability, but it also demonstrates the coach's commitment. One coaching session was in danger of going to waste when a colleague said, "Don't worry. She'll forget about it. She always does."

Good follow-up requires revisiting the agreed-upon action step within the agreed-upon time frame—"Did he or she accomplish X? If so, what is the next thing we will work on?"

Coaches should "tickle" action steps in their calendars and follow up on time. Follow-up is part of the focus and discipline. It is also an important part of role modeling. *If people know that the coach will follow up,* if they *expect* the coach to follow up, if they know the coach will not let things slide, if they believe the coach is on top of things, *they will perform better.*

In-the-Action Coaching

The six elements of the developmental coaching process can be used for full coaching sessions—20 to 30 minutes or more. They can also be used as the basis for on-the-spot coaching, which can take 2 to 8 minutes. When you find that you must coach in a hurry, ask:

- What is the problem?
- What are the obstacles?
- What can you do?

When you coach someone on the spot, do so in a way that allows the person to re-enter the action.

How Often to Coach

Coaching ideally can occur every day. And as a coaching culture develops, the job of coaching can extend beyond managers to peers coaching peers. Coaching happens in offices, in corridors, and on the run.

The coaching goals for a manager are:

- Coach every day during the action—this becomes a shorthand version of the developmental coaching process. But remember, the golden rule applies here: "They talk first."

- Set planned coaching meetings—these 20 to 30 minute meetings should occur on a timely basis near to the time of the event that has prompted the session. At an absolute *minimum,* these meetings should be held quarterly to make sure that things do not get too far out of range. An added value of a quarterly meeting with a salesperson is that it can help improve performance *before* it is too late, and it helps avoid the "big surprise" often associated with the annual performance assessment where the salesperson doesn't like the money or the message.

Basically, it is the coach's responsibility to call the quarterly coaching meeting, but the salesperson should also be encouraged to initiate the coaching session and take responsibility for his or her own development.

Everyday, Everyone Coaching

The whole developmental coaching process may seem time consuming. There is no doubt about it; it does take effort and it does take time. However, once a coach begins the coaching journey, this process takes on a life of its own and becomes second nature, and it becomes a fairly fast process. In summary: Open, uncover perceptions and needs, remove the obstacle, close, and follow-up. For a summary of Level 1, see Figures 3-1, 3-2, 3-3, and 3-4.

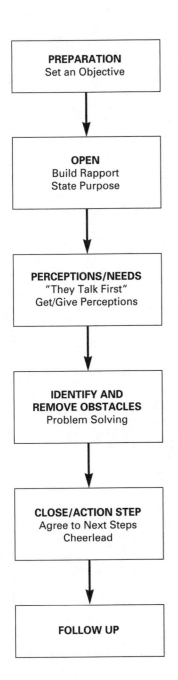

Figure 3-1   Level 1 at a glance.

Coaching Guidelines

PREPARATION
- ❑ Outline the objective(s).
- ❑ Prepare examples/feedback.
- ❑ Anticipate reaction and amount of time needed.

OPEN
- ❑ Build rapport — set tone.
- ❑ State purpose in nonjudgmental terms.
- ❑ Don't evaluate.
- ❑ Get ready to listen.

PERCEPTIONS/NEEDS
- ❑ Ask the salesperson to talk first about
  - ❑ perceptions of strengths.
  - ❑ areas for improvement.
- ❑ Question further to get salesperson to self-assess.
- ❑ Provide your perceptions with specific examples.
- ❑ Check perceptions.

IDENTIFY AND REMOVE OBSTACLES
- ❑ Two-way conversation will allow you to:
  - ❑ identify and agree on the obstacles.
  - ❑ get in-depth on a few critical issues.
  - ❑ ask salesperson to suggest options/ideas.
  - ❑ ask salesperson for desired outcome.
  - ❑ add value/discussion, examples, practice, demonstrations.

CLOSE/ACTION STEP
- ❑ Modify/agree on action step.
- ❑ Let salesperson summarize the action step.
- ❑ Agree on at least one developmental action step.
- ❑ Cheerlead/express hope for success; encourage the salesperson.
- ❑ Work toward partnership.
- ❑ Set up follow-up step.
- ❑ Decide if you should ask for feedback.

FOLLOW-UP
- ❑ Follow-up as agreed.

Figure 3-2   Level 1 checklist.

Coaching Guidelines	**Agenda**

PREPARATION
- ❑ Outline the objective(s).
- ❑ Prepare examples/feedback.
- ❑ Anticipate reaction and amount of time needed.

OPEN
- ❑ Build rapport — set tone.
- ❑ State purpose in nonjudgmental terms.
- ❑ Don't evaluate.
- ❑ Get ready to listen.

PERCEPTIONS/NEEDS
- ❑ Ask the salesperson to talk first about
  - ❑ perceptions of strengths.
  - ❑ areas for improvement.
- ❑ Question further to get salesperson to self-assess.
- ❑ Provide your perceptions with specific examples.
- ❑ Check perceptions.

IDENTIFY AND REMOVE OBSTACLES
- ❑ Two-way conversation will allow you to:
  - ❑ identify and agree on the obstacles.
  - ❑ get in-depth on a few critical issues.
  - ❑ ask salesperson to suggest options/ideas.
  - ❑ ask salesperson for desired outcome.
  - ❑ add value/discussion, examples, practice, demonstrations.

CLOSE/ACTION STEP
- ❑ Modify/agree on action step.
- ❑ Let salesperson summarize the action step.
- ❑ Agree on at least one developmental action step.
- ❑ Cheerlead/express hope for success; encourage the salesperson.
- ❑ Work toward partnership.
- ❑ Set up follow-up step.
- ❑ Decide if you should ask for feedback.

FOLLOW-UP
- ❑ Follow-up as agreed.

Figure 3-3 Developmental coaching planner.

Opportunities for Developmental Coaching

- Precall planning
- Postcall debriefing (windshield time)
- Pre- and postteam calling situations
- Improving performance of below-average performer
- Improving performance of average performer
- Improving performance of outstanding performer
- Solving a crisis/problem
- Motivating/empowering
- Teaching/training
- Troubleshooting
- Team calling

Figure 3-4   Developmental coaching opportunities.

Level 2—
the Art of Coaching:
Removing Obstacles

Level 1 of developmental coaching is like knowing the steps to a
dance. Level 2 puts the steps to music. Most managers do not
do developmental coaching at any level. That doesn't mean they
don't coach at all. It means that when they "coach," they usually
tell. Even managers who try to involve the person they are coaching, for example by asking, "How do you think it went?," usually find
themselves in a telling mode in a matter of moments. In Level 2 of
developmental coaching, the coach uses the process to achieve a
depth of understanding of what the salesperson's chief obstacle is.
It is about reaching that obstacle and removing it.

Asking questions will help the coach bring the obstacle to the
surface and get underneath it.

Coaching at Level 2 is truly coaching by asking. Questions are
the tools of Level 2: questions to identify obstacles, questions to
figure out options, and questions to arrive at outputs. For example,
the problem may be low numbers, but what is the obstacle? Is it
ability? Is it skill? Is it knowledge? Is it attitude? Is it effort? Or is it
a combination of these?

But Level 2 is much more than simply *asking* questions, as
evidenced by the following interchange (after a *second* team call
made by a manager and salesperson). After the first call, the man-

ager mentioned to the salesperson that he should build rapport and identify needs before "pitching the product." Practically the identical situation occurred again during the next team call. As you read this dialogue of the "coaching" session, bear in mind that the manager had been coached prior to the session to ask questions and listen, rather than tell. Notice that of five of the six comments the manager made, almost all were questions. Yet developmental coaching did *not* take place.

Here's how this coaching session went:

Dialogue	Critique
MANAGER: How do you think the call went? How effective were we?	Good start but could be better: Manager asked for perception of salesperson but made no statement of purpose.
SALESPERSON: Great. We are going to get the order.	
MANAGER: Well, do you remember the conversation we had after our last call when I said that there was a real need for you to ask more questions, and also to take some time on rapport?	Missed opportunity: Manager did not ask for specifics of what went well and what could have gone better. Manager did not find common ground. Manager used closed question.
SALESPERSON: *Very* vividly!	Salesperson seems resentful or sarcastic.
MANAGER: Do you see any similarities between that conversation and this call?	Not good: Manager is boxing salesperson into a corner.
SALESPERSON: Yes.	
MANAGER: What are they?	Waste/negative: Manager is grilling salesperson.

Dialogue	Critique
SALESPERSON: That rapport stuff and questioning. I think it's a little hokey. It can't help us make the numbers.	
MANAGER: Well, I'll tell you what. Do you think that more questions could have helped you do a better job?	Missed opportunity: Manager did not try to understand the obstacle. ("Hokey?" Why isn't it helpful in making the numbers?)
SALESPERSON: No. I think he'd ramble. I'm not convinced that rapport works.	
MANAGER: If you look at our corporate policy and other successful salespeople you'll see that is how we work here. Our policy....You will....	Boss, not coach: Manager pulled rank and resorted to "corporate policy."

This "coaching" session actually happened. How would you rate it? On the positive side, our manager did make a real attempt to question. But there are questions and there are questions. Some go for depth in a helpful way. Others sound like a prosecuting attorney. This coach clearly was the latter. But the salesperson was not in a court of law. None of the manager's five questions did anything to uncover or remove the salesperson's obstacle. Let's look to see what might have happened with questioning for depth.

Dialogue	Critique
COACH: That was really quite a call, wasn't it? I didn't even have time to call the office—that Smith project's really got us all running....	Better start: Rapport shows that the coach is a teammate.
SALESPERSON: Sure has.	
COACH: You know, Jay, at our last session we discussed rapport and questioning....Now while we're fresh from our call with Jones, I'd like to discuss the call and specifically look at these again. So how do you think the session went?	Good beginning: The coach states purpose and asks for the salesperson's perception.
SALESPERSON: Great! We are going to get the order.	
COACH: That's great! It's a good piece of business. What in particular leads you to think we'll get it?	Also good: The coach finds common ground and goes for depth.
SALESPERSON: Well, she said to call her tomorrow. She was also getting into specs. It sounds like a high sign to me. I also feel I was really ready to answer her questions and provide her with some solid information.	

Dialogue	Critique
COACH: Yes, those were positive signals, and you knew your stuff. I liked your explanation of (specifics). It was very clear.	Another plus: The coach states positives.
SALESPERSON: Thanks. I'm really excited about this opportunity.	
COACH: Good. I can tell. Now, Jay, looking back, what areas of the call do you think could have gone better? Where can we improve, in your view?	The coach uses questions to go deeper into the salesperson's perceptions and areas for improvement. The coach continues questioning to determine the obstacle.
SALESPERSON: Frankly, I can't see any area.	
COACH: What about rapport and questioning we discussed last time?	The coach continues using directive questions to determine the obstacle.
SALESPERSON: That rapport stuff and questioning. I think it's hokey. It can't help us make the numbers.	
COACH: What do you mean by "hokey" and that the rapport "can't help us make the numbers"?	The coach begins to make an important discovery: The obstacle seems to be related to an attitude about rapport—or perhaps a lack of relating skills or know-how in questioning. The coach must find what the resistance is all about. The coach is going for depth.

Dialogue	Critique
SALESPERSON: I feel Jones would either see right through it and clam up, or else she would jump at it and she'd start rambling and we'd never get to tell our story.	
COACH: Good points, Jay. You say Jones would see through it. What do you mean?...How can we make sure we have established rapport without being "hokey"? Questioning...?	Coach is ready to "tangle" *in a nondestructive way* on the importance of rapport and questions and challenge the salesperson's perceptions.

The salesperson is avoiding rapport and questioning. Why? What is his obstacle? Does he need help with the questions, how to ask them, build rapport in a genuine way? Finding the obstacle may seem like a "mystery" (that is exactly what one coach called it), but it is a mystery that can be solved with questioning. This is a philosophical question—how do people learn? John Locke, eighteenth-century English philosopher, believed that people are born with a tabula rasa—a "blank slate"—and that they must be instructed in what they don't know. The ancient Greek philosopher Plato held a different view. He believed that people were born with everything they needed to know and that the role of the teacher was to evoke this knowledge from inside them. Developmental coaching is based on the platonic view—that questioning is the key to helping people develop and grow based on what they know, helping them draw it out or figure it out.

Let's review some of the most compelling reasons to question rather than tell:

- The salesperson is more likely to respond to the coaching if he or she gets a say in it.

- Most salespeople prefer to be asked their perceptions as a part of the process.

- Questioning lets the coach uncover the salesperson's perception of the situation or problem.

- Optimal learning occurs when the salesperson is involved in the feedback and the problem solving.

- Involvement increases the commitment and buy-in to the solution by both the coach and the salesperson.

- The coach also has an opportunity to learn.

Approaches to coaching move on a continuum from directive—where the coach *tells* the person being coached about the situation/solution—to dialogue—in which the coach and the individual collaborate to understand the situation and identify the solution.

The coach has choices: He or she can do nothing, tell, or ask. In most situations this last choice is the best choice. The goals of any coaching session are to uncover the salesperson's perceptions and needs through in-depth questioning and to get the salesperson to identify and remove obstacles.

In-Depth Questioning

When asked for their perceptions of their performance, salespeople tend to give brief general answers or defer to their managers. But a coach can help salespeople self-assess by asking second and third questions to drill down—without sounding like a prosecuting attorney. For example, if a person says, "It went well. I think we'll get the contract," the coach can:

- *Ask why.* Why seems to be the most underutilized word in sales, and it is equally absent in coaching. "That's great. Why do you think we'll get the contract?"

- *Ask for a specific example.* "What specifically do you think went well?"

- *Ask a more directive question when the general question elicits little or no information.* Directive questions focus the salesperson's attention on the specific area the coach sees as the area for improvement. For example, if a coach feels that a particular proposal was unprofessional—with typos, incomplete text, or content errors—he or she could ask, "What do you think of the quality of the proposal we developed?" or "How do you think our proposal stacked up to...?" If product knowledge is the problem, the coach might ask, "How comfortable are you with your understanding of X product?" Or if a salesperson was inactive during a team call, the question might be, "How do you feel about your participation in the call?"

- *Dig deeper when the salesperson gives a fairly general answer.*

Most of all, the coach should *not* accept a salesperson's saying "I don't know" without making a *second effort*. The coach can push by saying, "Think about it. I'd like to know your view."

Positive Feedback

In addition to using questions to explore obstacles more deeply a coach can use questions to exploit positives as well. Praise is a great teacher. Great feedback is balanced, including both areas for improvement *and* strengths. When a salesperson fails to acknowledge his or her own strengths, the coach can ask for specifics on the positive side *and* take the time to give meaningful positive feedback. Spending 10 seconds on the positives and 20 minutes on the negatives is not balanced.

The Manager as Boss

One president of a very successful middle-market company said he did not agree with two aspects of the developmental coaching process. He took umbrage with the idea of giving positive feedback, and he totally resisted the idea that "They talk first." He explained that since he was president, it would hurt his integrity to act in this manner—"People know how I am. I'm not patient." He proceeded to describe how he would handle a coaching session. He cited an example of a sales manager who was not delegating. This is how he would coach:

> Mary, I'm concerned about your not delegating. Let me tell you what I think you need to do....You should....then....I want you to....It is vital that we....The system has....I feel....Is there anything you want to ask?

When we suggested that he try our approach (of positive feedback and her view first) one time, he said, "Absolutely not! I know the problem. She has what you would call a 'reverse fault.' She's a 'can-do' performer—it's actually one of her best strengths—but she also has to delegate!" We suggested that his natural insight was exactly what we were talking about, and we suggested that he use his instincts and still use an approach that is right for him:

> Mary, I'd like to discuss delegating with you. You have what I call a "reverse fault." It's actually one of your best strengths that you are *so* responsible and do so much (positive feedback). But I'm concerned you're doing things that you could delegate. How well do you think you are delegating? (Get her perception.)

The president was intrigued. "Hmmm. That is what I was thinking. But what if they don't come up with the right answer?" Well, maybe they won't, but at least they'll have a chance to *buy into* your answer.

In a training session with 40 managers, one of the managers, Mac, volunteered to play the role of coach in a role play. We set the situation as a team call. It was the second call in which Mac, the manager, would give feedback to Joe, the sales rep. Here's his attempt:

> MAC: Joe, I was very excited about your presentation. You honed into the product discussion. You have your product knowledge down pat. It seems like you went through the presentation *with* your peers before the meeting to prepare.
>
> I was, however, *very* disappointed with some aspects. Since our last team call, I *would have expected* that you would have *corrected* them. You didn't ask enough questions to find out how the customer was responding. The last time we discussed this you said questioning was a waste of time. But *I explained* how very, very important it is to get the customer's feelings and not just use your product knowledge.

At this point we stopped the role play. There were certain strengths in this presentation. Mac was direct, clear, articulate, and honest. He even started with praise. But when the managers in the seminar were asked to give Mac positive feedback, the best they could offer half jokingly was, "He refrained from a direct blow to the head." The number-one goal of the managers in this seminar was to "motivate" their salespeople—without money. They agreed that Mac's approach would fail to do that.

Then the group had a change of heart. They decided that since this was the second time Joe was given feedback on the subject, Mac's approach made sense. Using the seminar "time machine," we let the manager role-play that "first meeting." The results were revealing. The "first meeting" was a repeat of the first—with Mac doing all the talking, assessing, etc. The managers at the training session clearly saw that the process Mac used ("I tell") was not the result of the circumstances. Everyone agreed Mac needed to change his coaching style—except Mac.

One participant saw a way to get through to him. "Mac, you said to Joe, it's important to 'get the customer's feelings and not just your product knowledge.' That's a great point. How would you apply that to *Joe's* feelings?" Bingo. We then revisited the developmental coaching process and tied it to not only motivating people to *sell,* and to *improve the way* they sell, but also to role-model a need-based dialogue approach.

The main job of the coach is to help the person identify and remove his or her obstacles, and in-depth questioning is the way to do this. What are the possible obstacles? Is it skill or will? Here is a checklist:

- Does the person have the *capability?*
- Does the person have the *skill?*
- Does the person have the *knowledge?*
- Does the person have the *attitude?*
- Does the person make the *effort?*

There is almost no better way to figure this out than by using questions.

Here's a simple but powerful example of how in-depth questioning can get at an obstacle. In a seminar, a trainer asked participant 1 to ask participant 2 the question, "Do you like your job?" Participant 2 answered, "Yes. Yes, I do." The trainer asked participant 1 to repeat the question to participant 2. This time participant 2 responded, "Well, basically I do. I have autonomy and I like the people I work with. I like my work." "Ask again," the trainer said. This time, participant 1 said,

"That's enough." The trainer said, "No, it's not," and participant 1 asked the question again. Participant 2 responded: "Yes, I like my job, but I'm not challenged. I used to feel differently. Now I do the same things over and over. How many line sheets can you look at?…Every day I…; I would like to have some passion back in my work—feel excitement again."

What the group experienced was the power of *depth of questioning*. The questioner stayed with one question—"Do you like your job?" and repeated it three times. And through that an obstacle emerged. Each response was more complete, more thoughtful, more honest, and more meaningful. It takes skill to identify an issue and understand it!

Resolving Objections

It is very common during a coaching session—especially when the coach is going for depth—for the salesperson to resist. The resistance is usually aimed at one or both of two things:

- *The coaching process itself.* The salesperson may resist being made responsible for his or her own development. It is not uncommon for a coach to hear, "You're the boss; just tell me what you want and I'll do it." This can be a real trap for the coach.

- *The obstacle.* The salesperson may not acknowledge the obstacle, or may disagree about how to fix it. For example, one coach was faced with an objection when she suggested that the salesperson try again to meet with the decision maker. Although the salesperson agreed it was important to meet with the decision maker, he responded, "When my contact says no, there is nothing I can do. It is impossible. I can't go over his head."

This coach resisted the temptation to tell the salesperson what she knew—that she felt he was giving up too easily. The coach was convinced that the salesperson had failed to ask why his/her contact objected to arranging the meeting. But rather than act on her assumption, she coached. She was empathetic, saying she understood how he felt. Then she asked why it seemed impossible and what the salesperson could do to resolve it. As a result of this coaching, the sales rep came up with several effective uptiering tactics and felt prepared to leverage his contact to uptier.

Another trap in coaching is getting derailed from talking about the obstacle to talking about the *reasons or excuses* related (or not related) to the obstacle. The coach's role is to keep the focus on the obstacle *and what the person being coached can do that is in his or her control to overcome the obstacle.*

When salespeople object, it is up to the coach to avoid two things: flight (don't give up) and a fight (don't get defensive, attack). Instead, coaches should use the objection resolution process one would use to resolve a client objection:

- Empathy
- Question
- Position
- Check

For example:

> SALESPERSON: You're the manager. Just tell me what to do.
>
> COACH: I can see how you might feel that way. (*Empathy*) Why do you think that because of my role, I should tell you what to do? (*Question*)

Coaching takes strength—real emotional muscle. Unless coaches can hold their ground based on their belief that self-assessment is critical for development, they may be swayed and go along with the salespeople's program.

During the coaching session, the salesperson is likely to resent ideas put forth by the coach or become defensive about his or her position. For example, the salesperson might minimize a lost sale by saying, "Our pricing is too high." The natural tendency for the coach might be to respond by defending the pricing. More progress can be made by questioning, using the objection resolution process described earlier.

This model, by the way, is the same one salespeople should use with their customers who object. And in using it, the coach not only can help resolve this sales problem but role model good client-focused selling. Example:

Dialogue	*Comment*
SALESPERSON: Our pricing is too high.	*Don't* contradict, argue, rebut, snap back, or agree; *do* show concern and regard for the individual's point of view.
COACH: I understand that our pricing is a concern. What are you comparing it to in saying it is too high?	Show *empathy.* Question to uncover need.
SALESPERSON: X is providing a discount and that's impossible to fight!	
COACH: Well let's think about that _____. Let's look at their total package. What else….What do we really know about the competitor's total offering and price?…What do we offer comparably?…How are you responding to price objections?…What can you do now?	Make comparisons.

Dialogue	*Comment*
SALESPERSON: I can call X...compare...show...offset....I have to find out if X guarantees....I'll....	
COACH: Based on..., what do you think?	Get feedback and agreement to action step.

Six Critical Skills

As in the selling process, skills help a coach develop a coaching dialogue. And just as a salesperson can use skills to identify client needs and move the sale forward to the close, the coach uses skills to create a dialogue with his or her salespeople. We have identified six critical skills (see Figure 4-1):

```
┌─────────────────┐
│    Presence     │
└─────────────────┘

┌─────────────────┐
│    Rapport      │
└─────────────────┘

┌─────────────────┐
│   Questioning   │
└─────────────────┘

┌─────────────────┐
│   Listening     │
└─────────────────┘

┌─────────────────┐
│   Positioning   │
└─────────────────┘

┌─────────────────┐
│    Checking     │
└─────────────────┘
```

Figure 4-1   Six critical skills at a glance.

- *Presence.*   How confident yet approachable is the coach?

- *Rapport.*   Does the coach take time to recognize the salesperson as a person? Is the coach friendly—hard on measurement, but soft on people?

- *Questioning.*   How well does the coach ask questions? How skilled is the coach in asking questions and following up on the salesperson's answers with more questions to go deeper?

- *Listening.*   How good a listener is the coach? Can the coach find common ground as a way to build a bridge with the salesperson? Does the coach pick up and integrate the salesperson's view and language into his or her comments?

- *Positioning.*   How well does the coach integrate what he or she hears from the salesperson with his or her ideas? How well does the coach focus on benefits to the salesperson?

- *Checking.*   How well does the coach ask for feedback and keep the dialogue going?

The developmental coaching process closely parallels the consultative selling process—identifying needs before positioning solutions or ideas. One of the best aspects of the developmental coaching process is that as the coach uses it, she or he role-models need-based selling skills.

Level 3—
the Heart of Coaching

Since the process of developmental coaching runs counter to how most managers and salespeople have experienced coaching, mastering it requires a commitment to change. Developmental coaching is effective because it starts with a belief in the innate value and integrity of people. The aim is progress, not perfection—there is *always* a next level. The beauty of developmental coaching is that it ultimately leads to self-development for the coach and for the person being coached. Salespeople learn how to identify their own obstacles and take responsibility for removing them.

The big payoff for coaches is that their people will continue to improve. The process of developmental coaching creates buy-in and commitment. And when one realizes that most people will do what they want to do, buy-in and commitment are all the more precious.

The coach-as-resource model positions the manager not as a be-all and end-all "expert" but as a part of a development continuum: "I know. You know. Others know. Let's all figure it out and know more." The expert model fits well into top-down hierarchy; the resource model fits well in the Stretch Zone. A coach can create a peer dynamic and a supportive environment where people are open to feedback. When the coach is truly committed to helping everybody get better, trust and commitment follow.

If Level 1 is the process of coaching and Level 2 is the art of coaching, then Level 3 is its heart. For someone to open up and reveal problems (obstacles), there needs to be a level of trust. Level 3 of coaching is the level of partnership, since it is based on trust and the belief that the coach is there to help.

All levels of coaching take time. In the long run, though, they *save* time because salespeople truly get better and better. The key is for managers to prepare for their sessions, coach, and self-critique and/or ask for feedback for themselves.

Level 3 is all about building trust and strengthening the relationship between the coach and the salesperson. Trust cannot be achieved in an environment in which people feel fear or believe they have to watch their backs. In an environment of fear, far from engaging in open and honest dialogue, people filter what they say. In such an environment, feedback is very limited, and growth is limited, too.

Trust builds incrementally. Every contact between a manager and a salesperson has the potential to change their relationship. The good news is that each contact can make the relationship better. The bad news is that it can also make it worse.

If in each coaching session a manager forces the salesperson into a passive role, causing him or her to feel incompetent or trapped into responding only in the way the coach expects, over time the relationship will deteriorate. The person will gradually become demotivated or resentful—or worse yet, try to set up a team against the coach. Revenge can take subtle or overt forms— from not completing work to acting out or being confrontational with the coach or others.

At Level 3 the coach and salesperson are a team. The salesperson's integrity is intact, and he or she becomes active and responsible for his or her own learning. This is the very opposite of the negative situation in which the person being coached winds up feeling stupid. It is also better than a "motivational pep talk," which is a temporary fix at best.

Many people feel motivation is an ideal state—hence the familiar line, "Motivate my people!" But, in fact, while motivation is good and certainly much better than demotivation, it is a middle ground. In traditional motivational coaching people are told what to do. The "motivation" comes from an external force. It is often based on an "if this, then that"/carrot-or-stick approach in which behaviors are a contingency. Furthermore, the motivational approach usually requires raising the ante (more carrots, bigger sticks). Often when the carrots or the sticks stop coming, the motivation often goes away too.

Motivational coaching can lead to a flat-line effect: While it often avoids the valleys, it misses the peaks. There is a way to get to and sustain higher ground. That way is developmental coaching, which empowers both the coach and the person being coached. With developmental coaching the coach's goal is to help take valleys and flip them to peaks and maintain the peaks to create higher ones. At Level 3 this is possible because a strong relationship exists between the coach and salesperson.

How to Strengthen the Relationship

The goal of every coaching session should be to strengthen the relationship while removing the obstacle.

- Discuss the salesperson's needs.

  Consider the needs of the salesperson being coached.

  Solicit needs rather than imposing them (ideally).

  Ask how you and the salesperson can best work together.

- Discuss your needs.

  Discuss how you need the salesperson to contribute to strengthening the relationship over time.

  Discuss how you would like to best work with the salesperson.

- Determine a plan to add value to one another.

  Help the individual see how to use the feedback to grow—ask, "What can you/we learn from this?"

  Determine operating practices that will be beneficial to both of you. Create a win-win situation.

- Have a relationship meeting.

In addition to your coaching around specific sales topics, it is very helpful to set a separate meeting to ask: "What do we need to do differently (that we can control) to make our relationship stronger?" or "What am I doing that is getting in your way?" or "What can I do to be more helpful?" This discussion should take place at least one time per year when no other topic is on the table. (See Figure 5-1.)

Relationship Meeting

One time per year,
when nothing else is on the table,
ask:

*"What am I doing
that is getting in
your way?"*

Figure 5-1 Relationship meeting.

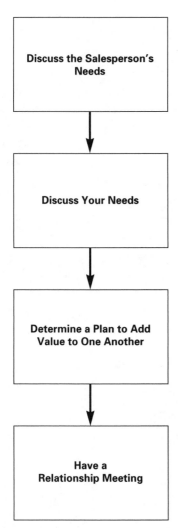

Figure 5-2   Level 3 at a glance.

See Figure 5-2 for a summary of Level 3.

Before moving on to peer coaching, self-coaching, and coaching the team, let's think about three aspects of the developmental coaching process for managers: phone coaching, team-call coaching, and consequence coaching.

Phone Coaching, Team-Call Coaching, and Consequence Coaching

Phone Coaching

With geographic expansion, the sales playing field is going "electronic." The rise of the virtual office/home office has created a new set of management challenges. Organizations with remote salespeople are struggling to find ways to support them to reduce the isolation and detachment that are common by-products of being out of touch. Organizations are seeking ways to support and retain salespeople who are on their own most of the time. Without support, at best, an organization will have a group of independent salespeople who will not feel or act like they are a part of the team.

Remote salespeople demand a tighter structure with very clear boundaries. For example, they need a few strong principles around things like values ("go crazy" for clients) and levels of authority (parameters). One of the most important things the coach can do is work with the salespeople to determine how corporate can add value. Remote salespeople need a strong base that will serve as a driving force for them. They need technology and the skill to apply the technology to their business. And they need coaching.

The telephone, voice mail, e-mail, conference calls, and in some organizations video conferencing can literally become life-lines to keep salespeople connected, plugged in, and "on."

To leverage the power of the phone, a coach should be aware of the advantages and drawbacks of the phone as a coaching tool. On the positive side, the phone allows for immediacy and convenience. It provides a way to reach out. It even offers some distance, both physical and mental, which at times can be a good thing. On the negative side, there are a number of issues. First, it is harder to establish or maintain rapport by phone, since there is no "personal contact." It is also more difficult to "read" the situation without body language. Both the coach and the salesperson can, because it is by phone, minimize the importance of what is being covered. These factors make it all the more important to use the developmental coaching process. The biggest problem is the manager who does not call unless there is a problem, does not return calls, and does not encourage calls.

Let's look at some dos and don'ts.

Dos

- Make a coaching appointment or at least check if it is a good time to talk. Keep the appointment! Have start and stop times and stick to them.

- Prepare—it's easy to forget to cover things: Make an agenda, keep a list in front of you and take notes!

- Fax materials in advance if you have a document you will be referring to or if you will need the materials during a coaching session.

- Keep a positive tone of voice.

- Use the developmental coaching model.

Begin with brief rapport. State your purpose...end with a next step.

Use the six critical skills, particularly checking to get feedback. Keep the dialogue going. Don't assume silence means agreement.

- If you must leave a message or voice mail, use your judgment and be sensitive. Be aware that someone else may hear the message or the person for whom you leave the message at that point can't respond to you.

- Periodically ask, "How can we improve these coaching sessions?"

- Expand your horizons: Use the phone, voice mail, and e-mail to communicate positives, thank-yous, and good lucks for upcoming calls and to congratulate a salesperson on a success.

- Leave a phone number and a time you can be reached.

- Make a relationship call—ask how the salesperson is doing, what he or she needs.

- Return calls ASAP and always within 12 hours.

Don'ts

- Don't just cover the negatives. Balance your feedback. Consider the salesperson picking up your message as he or she returns from an 11:00 p.m. flight after a long day and flight delays.

- Don't assume you have all the information. Don't tell; ask.

- Don't cover personal or really serious topics on the phone if you have any possible alternative. If you must, set a phone appointment and state that you wish you could be having the discussion in person.

- Don't automatically use the speakerphone. If you must, keep your voice soft; don't shout. Over a speakerphone, voices come across more harshly.

- *Don't* use voice mail or fax when you are angry. If you are upset, you will leave a message that can do a lot of damage—much worse than a face-to-face situation where dialogue is possible.

Voice Mail—Danger

As for using voice mail as a coaching tool, *when in doubt, don't.* And when you do, do so with care. Like any one-way communication mode (others include memos, e-mail, or faxes), voice mail lacks that essential dimension of communication known as feedback. Keep in mind that you are not there to temper or explain your message and that you may not have all the facts and conditions. Also, since the salesperson cannot respond on the spot, he or she may become frustrated and unnecessarily upset. Not every voice mail system has a "check your message" feature, and you may not be able to edit your message. One manager who was frustrated with the way certain seniors in his organization were using voice mail called it their "one-way assertion tool." Nevertheless, when used with judgment and skill, voice mail can be a real asset.

Plan what you will say, positives and negatives. If you are not prepared to leave a balanced message, hang up! Don't coach over voice mail if you are very upset. The anger you feel will come through, and the person won't hear anything else.

One inappropriate voice mail message pushed a senior manager to resign. The manager received the message at the end of a long day that began with a morning meeting. At that meeting, she sat quietly as her junior colleague presented an important report. Her strategy was to give this colleague a chance to build his credibility. Later that day, her boss, who had been in the meeting, left a stinging message that she picked up at 9:30 p.m. "Jean, I was very disappointed in your performance at the meeting. You sat there while Bob did all the talking. You should have had a stronger role. I'm upset about your judgment!" For her it was the "straw that broke the camel's back." This is a perfect example of how not to "coach." He might have at least asked, "Jean, please give me a call. I'd like to discuss your thinking in having Bob do the presenting."

Phone coaching can and does work. A coach can use phone coaching to support a sales team, build their skills, and strengthen the relationships.

Team-Call Coaching

Team selling and team delivery have become a strategy for many organizations. Team selling is an excellent way to leverage resources and expand relationships with clients. It allows an organization to match its resources to the client needs. A team call with the sales manager and sales person shows bench strength, and it provides a great vehicle for teaching and coaching.

Preparation

Preparation is vital if the team is to maximize the potential of the call. Without preparation, the team will not look and act like a team. When team members do prepare it is usually about the technical aspects of the call, not the team process or the call strategy. It is the coach's responsibility to set the expectations for the preparation for the team call, but it is the salesperson's responsibility to fulfill the expectations.

The discussion should include:

- The objective of the team call (why are we meeting?)
- Roles (who will do what? what part of the agenda? time?)
- Client contacts (who will be there?)
- Client expectations and needs (what does the client want?)
- Client background (what is known about the client's strategy, business, industry, and needs?)
- Competitors (who are the competitors? how do you stack up?)

- Status of relationship (what is the present position—strengths? vulnerabilities?)

- Sensitivities (what are the hot issues from the last call?)

- Strategy/agenda for the call (what ideas and products will be discussed?)

- Key questions to ask

- Anticipated objections

- Desired action step/close (what will we want the client or prospect to do as a result of the call?)

The sales call planner and the team call planner, found at the end of this book, can be helpful tools. Salespeople should complete them prior to the precall meeting with the coach. An effective precall meeting with the coach can take as little as five minutes if there is a clear process for call preparation and an expectation of coaching.

During the Call

In a team call with a salesperson, unless it is a "senior to senior" meeting explicitly set for that purpose, the manager role is to support the relationship with the salesperson. Without a coach "mentality," managers can subtly and unintentionally undermine the credibility of their salespeople by "taking over" or by introducing a junior person in a way that destroys his or her credibility. One leading organization gave its senior team a two-hour session in note taking after losing a deal. The reason they lost the deal: the arrogant way one of the seniors spoke to his junior. His directive, "Write that down so *you'll* remember to do it," confirmed the client's fear that once the business was won the junior would do all the work. In almost all situations a good coach does not "take over" but knows how to "turn it over."

Here are some don'ts and dos:

Don'ts

- Don't "hog" the call.

  CLIENT: Well, what can your company do for us?

  MANAGER (jumping in): Well, first of all it seems...then we offer...which matches your....

- Don't take over.

  MANAGER (interrupting salesperson): Yes, yes, and in my view....

Dos

- Defer to the salesperson.

  CLIENT: Tom (manager), what do you think...will do?

  COACH: Bob (salesperson), you've been looking into that. What do you think? *or* Why don't you describe...?

- Include the salesperson in the discussion and next steps:

  CLIENT: Tom, when can we expect to see...?

  COACH: Bob and I will look into that and....

- Go out with salespeople *to support them.*

After the Call

It is absolutely essential to debrief after every team call, no matter how briefly. Fairly quickly this becomes second nature, and the call debriefing can be quick, almost done in shorthand. The higher the trust, the faster and deeper the debriefing. Use the developmental coaching process to help the salesperson self-coach. (They talk first. Start with positives, then areas for improvement. Go deep on one or two things. And don't forget to follow up!) The coach should also self-critique and, most important, ask the salesperson for feedback. Finally, the debriefing should be on the process and skills, not just on the deal or content of the call. (See the sales critique checklist in the Appendix for a call debriefing tool.)

Consequence Coaching

As all coaches know, there are people who won't perform, regardless of what kind of support and developmental coaching they are given. *Consequence coaching* is a derivative form of developmental coaching that helps address ongoing performance problems. Figure 6-1 contrasts developmental and consequence coaching.

Developmental Coaching Process	Consequence Coaching Process

• *Preparation*
  • Coach and salesperson outline objective
	• *Preparation*
	  • Coach outlines objective

• *Opening*
  • Coach establishes rapport
  • Coach states purpose
	• *Opening*
	  • Coach establishes rapport
	  • Coach states purpose

• *Perceptions/needs*
  • Salesperson talks first
	• *Perceptions/needs*
	  • Coach talks first and does not ask for salesperson's perceptions (since that has been done sufficiently)

Figure 6-1 Developmental versus consequence coaching.

Developmental Coaching Process	Consequence Coaching Process

• *Identifying and removing the obstacles*
    • Salesperson identifies obstacles and options to remove them
    • Coach edits options as necessary
	• *Identifying and removing the obstacles*
	    • Coach states current situation and what is expected, by when, and consequences of standards not being met
	    • Coach practices, demonstrates, etc.

• *Close/action step(s)*
    • Salesperson summarizes
    • Salesperson agrees to objectives/next steps
    • Coach expresses hope for success
	• *Close/action step(s)*
	    • Salesperson summarizes
	    • Coach checks and summarizes
	    • Salesperson agrees to objectives/next steps
	    • Coach expresses hope for success

• *Following up*
    • Both coach and salesperson are responsible for follow-up
	• *Following up*
	    • Both coach and salesperson are responsible for follow-up
	    • Coach documents the meeting

Figure 6-1   *(Continued)*

As its name suggests, the objective of this coaching session is to spell out in no uncertain terms the standards the salesperson is required to meet and the consequences of failing to meet them. Consequence coaching is the step to take after developmental coaching has been exhausted. It is in consequence coaching, and only consequence coaching, that the three guiding words "They talk first" do not apply. At this stage, the coach does not ask the salesperson for his or her perception, since that has already been done, usually several times over, prior to this stage.

Consequence coaching is a convergence of developmental coaching and evaluative coaching. It is developmental in its support aspect, and it is evaluative in its grading aspect. In the consequence session, the coach states his or her perception of where things stand, and what is unacceptable. Then the coach states the standards the person must meet, when he or she has to meet them, and the *consequences* of not meeting them. The person being coached must clearly understand his or her expectations, what he or she is not doing, what needs to happen, and what the consequences will be if this does not happen. Depending on the situation, the person can be placed informally or formally on notice. Before this meeting, it is advisable for the coach to get guidance from the human resource group.

Evaluative Coaching —Performance Assessment

U p to this point the focus has been on development. Now let's look in depth at evaluation. *Evaluative coaching* is coaching that makes up performance reviews. This is when the coach puts on his or her evaluative hat. It is safe to say that few if any professionals look forward to performance reviews—whether they are being reviewed or doing the reviewing.

But performance reviews can become a powerful force if developmental (ongoing) and evaluative (one to four times a year) coaching are linked as a total process.

Many factors have made the performance review a dreaded event in corporate life for coaches and their people alike. First, even in organizations where they try to separate things, money and job security are attached to it. Moreover, many people are getting feedback for the first and final time in the period evaluated— usually an entire year! The great challenge is to get past the reality of pay and position and make the performance review into something different, something positive. This starts with changing the mindset that sees feedback as something negative. Without good feedback, it is impossible to use the performance review as a means for ongoing improvement—for both the coach and his or her salespeople.

Developmental feedback has improvement as its singular goal. Evaluative feedback has two goals: first and foremost to make sure that the person whose performance is being reviewed has a clear picture of how he or she is *perceived* and *rated*—whether the rating is from the coach/managers, peers, or other team members or a composite of all of these (the 360-degree evaluation mentioned earlier). The person being reviewed gets a score of some kind.

The second objective is to begin the developmental process so the picture *improves* for the next evaluative session. In a performance review, about 90 percent of the time should be dedicated to giving the person being evaluated a clear picture of the past and a score or ranking to help quantify the picture. The other 10 percent ideally should be devoted to what the person must do to get a better score next time/next year or to improve and develop. Sometimes people are upset about the money, rating, position, security, and so on. In this case, it may be best to merely introduce the idea of development and set a second meeting the next day or next week—not as long as next month—to begin developmental coaching.

In a year-end meeting at the chairman level, a senior manager complained that one region was significantly behind in its collections. Another senior manager warned, "The performance appraisal is coming up (in May and it was January) and it will be corrected then." Perhaps this manager was right and collections should be key criteria in the performance review, but his comment was very telling. Fortunately, the new head of human resources put things into perspective, "Are you saying we won't do anything about this until four months from today in May when we do performance reviews?" He made the point perfectly that feedback given during performance reviews does no more than deliver a grade for past performance. It would do nothing to change the performance of those four months.

Evaluative feedback is necessary because it lets the person see how he or she is perceived. Every salesperson has the right to this information. Of course, the more open and trusting the relationship between the coach and the salesperson, the more open the salesperson will be to the information. And this is often directly related to the quantity and quality of ongoing coaching that precedes the performance review. The better and more consistent the developmental coaching, the greater the chance for a more positive performance review, since there will be almost no surprises or recriminations.

Role of the Coach

The role of the coach in a performance review is to be the messenger—to deliver an *evaluative message* for his or her *organization* so that the salesperson knows where he or she stands relative to his or her performance. This is when coaches don their manager hats. Most managers are not very good at this kind of feedback. For example, one young salesperson was very upset with her raise. Based on the feedback she had gotten she said, "I thought I was doing great." The manager replied, "Great for you, but not in comparison." The message must reflect the coach's as well as the organization's perception of the person up to that point in time. It can also include peer and team feedback if the organization has instituted 360-degree feedback. When this is the case, the coach should synthesize the information from his or her own feedback and that of the organization to provide comparative data relative to others in the organization.

Regardless of how hard it is to "paint the picture," it is the coach's responsibility to paint it so that the person being evaluated fully understands how he or she is rated. Although it is not essential that the person agree with it, it is essential that he or she understand it.

The information provided in a performance review is vital because it lets the salesperson know what to work on to get better and succeed. As mentioned earlier, the "score" can be a number, grade, quartile, or scale. A scale that is associated with the big picture is very helpful in that it allows salespeople to understand clearly how they rated and where they stand relative to others.

Since a performance review is so important, let's look at the two critical success factors of a successful performance review:

- Preparation
- The performance review meeting

Preparation

Preparation for the performance review is a must if the coach is to be fair to the salesperson.

Preparation begins with understanding the objectives of the performance review. There are four objectives:

- The coach gets the salesperson's perception
- The coach gives his or her perception
- The coach gives the perception of the organization formally including peer feedback, or informally with general impressions
- The coach begins the developmental coaching process

The coach should be certain about the assessment and be prepared to back it up with specific examples to help paint the picture clearly. It is the task of the coach to present not only his or her view but the organization's view. The coach must make it clear the review is a *composite* of many views—not just the coach's own. The organization's view is a significant factor even if it is general. Often salespeople object to peer reviews, saying they are unfair.

They often say that they value only the feedback of the coach. When this happens, it is essential for the coach to support broader feedback and to reinforce that in the organization other views also count.

Of course the coach must be able to represent peer reviews in a credible way. When one coach was told one of the salespeople on his team wasn't "crisp," he went to the reviewer and asked "Why? What is the criteria? What is the impact? What are some examples?" If a coach has any confusion about a part of the picture anyone paints, it is his or her job to go to the source and ask what it means. If someone ranks a salesperson as being in the X quartile and the coach isn't clear, the coach should go back and ask about it, so he or she can represent it accurately.

The coach should give the salesperson ample time to prepare for the meeting so that he or she is ready to discuss his or her performance. Preparation is the obligation of the coach and salesperson. If at all possible, a week prior to the meeting, the coach should ask the salesperson being evaluated to do a self-evaluation. This allows the salesperson to really think about his or her own performance in greater depth. Some organizations have tools or forms that they use. This often makes the meeting much easier because often people are harder on themselves than the coach is. The coach should prepare by gathering his or her data and begin to formulate a score.

Performance reviews are emotional times. The coach needs to make sure his or her own discomfort about being reviewed and his or her own attitudes about feedback don't get in the way of giving each person a clear and helpful performance review.

As a part of preparation the coach should take care of the logistics:

- Where to meet? Whenever possible, the ideal place would be a neutral spot other than the coach's own office. One coach used a small conference room as a neutral place and sat next to his salesperson. These symbols created a collegial environment. This coach knew he had authority and didn't need to reinforce it. If his or her office is the best choice, the coach should avoid sitting behind his or her desk to help reinforce a more collegial feeling.

• How much time? The coach should schedule enough time to have a full conversation. One coach really sent the wrong signals when he took phone calls during the performance review. And when he *started* the meeting *by saying* "We have one-half hour," he pretty much closed down communications. In general, about 30 to 45 minutes should be adequate.

The Performance Review Meeting

The performance review is divided into two parts. The first—and major—part is the evaluative part. The evaluative part of the performance review is obviously important. It should take up *at least* 90 percent of the meeting. The second part (if the coach gets into it—and there is a choice) is the beginning of the developmental feedback part. See Figure 7-1 for a performance review checklist.

The key elements of a performance review meeting are

• Preparation

• Opening

• Perceptions

• Rating

• Summary

• Close

• The developmental segment (optional)

The Performance Review Process

Preparation

- Coach
- Salesperson's self-assessment

Opening—coach states objectives

- To present a picture of strengths and areas for improvement
- To discuss how to make next year better

Perceptions

- Salesperson's perceptions
- Coach's perceptions

Rating

- Salesperson's rating
- Coach's rating

Summary

- Salesperson summarizes what he or she got out of the meeting

Close—next steps are agreed to

The developmental segment (optional):

- Begin development/performance plan for the new year, or
- Set a time to meet to begin the development and performance plan for the next year

---

Figure 7-1 Performance review checklist.

Phase One—the Evaluative Segment

Opening

The coach should set a *dual* purpose:

- First, "I am going to 'paint a picture' of what others see and what I see in your performance, both areas of strength and areas for improvement," or, "I'm going to present the evaluation....It is a 'snapshot' of the last year (quarter)." "I hope you find that it's a pretty good likeness—of both your strengths and weaknesses."

- "Then we will talk about next year and how to make it better. This is very important, and we can cover this today or we can set a second meeting."

One coach really started fireworks when he began by saying "You're a three." Do *not* open with the number or grade.

Perceptions

As in developmental coaching, it is the coach's job to deliver the message. But how he or she does it is *everything.*

- Take a moment for rapport.
- Get the salesperson's perceptions, and ask for his or her self-rating. Ask why? Again, remember: "They talk first!" One coach was amazed at how much this helped. In advance of the meeting the coach had asked the salesperson to think about her performance for the year. He asked her to look at two things:
  - What did she do well? He directed her to discuss positives first even though she wanted to get to negatives.
  - What are her areas for improvement?

When the coach asked for her perception, even though in this case he disagreed with much of what she said, this information allowed him to paint his picture more intensely because he saw *her* picture. He was able to contrast where necessary and create a dialogue.

The evaluative process looks like this:

- The salesperson describes/paints a picture of positives.
- The coach describes/paints a picture of his or her perceptions of the positives.
- The salesperson describes/paints a picture of areas for improvement.
- The coach gives areas for improvement.

Rating

The salesperson gives his or her view of the total picture—a self-rating. The coach should ask the salesperson to give his or her grade or score. When the grade or rating suggested by this salesperson is aligned with the sales manager's rating of the salesperson, the session is more likely to move into the developmental segment.

The coach then gives his or her rating. He or she gives the rating or grade and discusses it.

Summary

Now, the coach asks the salesperson to summarize to make sure the message is clear—even if it is not necessarily agreed with. The coach should ask the person being evaluated to summarize what happened. What did he or she get out of the meeting?

Close (or Move into Developmental Segment)

The coach then asks the salesperson if he or she wishes to move into the development phase to discuss how to make the next year better. If the answer is no, the coach should get agreement on next steps and then set the date for the development/performance plan meeting. The coach could ask for feedback on what he or she can do to help and on what the organization can do. The coach should wrap up the session with a thank-you.

Phase Two—the Developmental Segment (Salesperson's Choice)

The coach and salesperson can determine whether the session should move into the developmental phase. If so, this should make up no more than 10 percent of the meeting. To decide whether to get into the developmental part, the coach should ask the salesperson being evaluated. The coach should respect the salesperson's decision either by going into the developmental feedback part of the meeting or by setting up another meeting for the next day or next week.

When a review hasn't been positive, the coach can ask, "Are you up for the developmental discussion to help make next year's picture better?" Even if the session has been great, people may be too exhilarated about their positives to focus on areas of improvement then and there. One coach was surprised when one of his top performers declined when he asked him if he were in the mood to think about development. The coach respected this and said, "Fine. Let's set time in the next week to talk about making next year better...."

If the salesperson *is* ready, the coach and salesperson can discuss how to make the next year better and set a time to create the performance plan for next year.

If the salesperson wishes to begin the developmental part, the coach can begin that with the comment, "Let's take a look at what we need to accomplish next year," to help the salesperson think about objectives for the next year and to begin a performance and development plan. In all likelihood the creation of the performance plan for the following year should begin at the next meeting after the salesperson has had the chance to work on his or her plan. The performance plan for the next year then becomes the template and criteria for the performance evaluation for that period of time. The best advice for developing a performance plan is keep it objective, clear, and simple.

General Guidelines for a Performance Review

Two rules of thumb are

- Be honest. Don't hedge.
- Ask questions. Don't do all the talking.

  Other guidelines include

- If the meeting is going badly, end it. Acknowledge that it is going badly. Discuss this. If it can't be turned around, reschedule!
- Don't start with the hardest point first. Start with positives.
- Don't think of the meeting as leading up to a big bang. If you do developmental coaching all year, this won't be traumatic or shocking!
- Be positive about the performance review and feedback. Your attitude sets the tone.

Avoid the three biggest mistakes:

- *Don't be unprepared.*

- *Don't forget to set the dual purpose in the opening.* Give a score and set a plan to make things better, even better for the next review.

- *Don't change your grade.* Sometimes you may do this, but only rarely—2 percent of the time. You would have to be *so* very off that you need to go back and change your picture because it is not accurate. It is not okay to change your review if you are off only 5 percent. Preparation is key. Differences and disappointments are almost inevitable, but with proper preparation, the coach can be fair and accurate.

Coach's Self-critique after the Performance Review

The coach should self-critique after each session:

- Did I pave the way for this session with ongoing developmental coaching?

- What did I do well in this session?

- What can I do better next time?

- Am I asking for feedback at least one time per year—"What am I doing in my control that is getting in your way?"

- Is my attitude positive about performance reviewv s?

- Did I set a time for the developmental meeting after the performance review?

Mindset

As with developmental coaching, skill is only one part of being an effective evaluator. The other part is mindset and attitude. If the coach has negative feelings about performance evaluation, that negativity will be projected. Salespeople have a right to see a clear picture of how they are perceived. Not getting feedback can hurt their careers. It can hold them back. The coach is the tool—not the cause and not the source—of learning. It is the coach's job to be as effective and helpful as he or she can be, and this takes attitude, skill, and the effort to consistently provide developmental and evaluative coaching.

Sales Meetings
—Coaching the Team

We have focused on coaching between two people, coach-to-salesperson. But a coach also has the opportunity to coach his or her team. In a team setting the coach can role-model coaching and encourage peers to coach peers. The sales meeting is an excellent setting for coaching the team.

Let's focus on maximizing the sales meeting. Based on our experience with hundreds of sales managers, many sales meetings—whether they are held weekly, monthly, or quarterly—turn out to be predominantly administrative in nature. This is a phenomenon not unrelated to the fact that most of the coaching that goes on is evaluative. Most are primarily one-way meetings in which the manager or a designated person assumes a dominant role of telling. Much of what gets covered could be covered in a memo.

These kinds of meetings do not begin to touch the true potential of what can be achieved when the team is together. The real power is the interaction and synergy that can be created. One-on-one coaching sessions are great, but there is one thing they cannot do: They cannot help build the team. Although a coach can help build the skills of individual salespeople one-on-one, the coach cannot build a team one-on-one. Effective sales meetings are a great place to build group commitment and provide a forum for team members to share know-how and solve problems together.

The coach needs a team if salespeople's jobs are interrelated. Sales meetings are a perfect arena for building selling skills and fostering peer coaching around real situations and issues. In a meeting setting, it is possible to make the whole greater than its parts. Like basketball players, individual team members can be developed one-on-one, but a team needs to practice together.

It is not the content of most sales meetings that is the problem. For example, typical topics might include things such as differentiating against the competition, cross-selling, resolving tough objections, generating new business, solving pricing issues, building skills, creating strategies, reaching new markets, and so on. In general it is the process, the dynamics of how the topics are covered, that is the problem.

Attitudes toward Sales Meetings

Let's begin by thinking about how most people feel about weekly or monthly sales meetings. Unfortunately, few salespeople or even sales managers really look forward to them. Many dread them. The most common complaints about meetings, sales or otherwise, are consistent:

- They are a waste of time.
- Nothing gets accomplished.
- The wrong people participate.
- Some people dominate.
- Others don't participate at all.
- Many people don't know why they are there.
- Last but not least, the meetings are boring.

Meetings in general are so suspect that two companies we know of have created chair-free conference rooms with the sole intention of keeping meetings short.

Lack of Know-how

Even sales managers who are effective in one-on-one coaching situations can find themselves at a loss in a meeting environment. This isn't surprising, since the dynamics and challenges are very different. For example, a comment that can be a toss-away in a one-on-one situation can be devastating in a group setting, and staying focused in a conversation with one salesperson is much different from doing the same thing with six people in a room. A second set of skills is called for. Whereas one-on-one coaching skills form the basis for communication, leading a meeting effectively demands group presentation skills, team-building skills, and meeting skills.

The developmental coaching process for one-on-one coaching forms the cornerstone of effective, successful sales meetings, but it takes more. Coaches need to master a process for leading a *meeting*. A coach needs know-how: understanding how to control the meeting, how to get participation, how to get commitment, and how to handle interpersonal issues—all in a group setting. Most of the classic objections to meetings can be resolved by a coach who knows how to optimize—not dominate—the group.

Some of the most common questions managers ask about how to lead effective meetings are:

- How long and how often should I run sales meetings?
- How can I get participation?
- How can I keep the meeting on track and avoid going off on tangents?

- How can I make the meeting productive?

- How do I get through all of the topics we have to cover?

- How can I quiet down the extroverts and bring out the nontalkers?

- How can I control the meeting without sacrificing spontaneity?

- How can I see that decisions are carried out after the meeting?

- How can I cope with different objectives and different needs all at one time?

- How can I get the salesforce to feel ownership for the meeting?

- Who should lead the sales meeting?

- How can I deal with personality problems?

Not surprisingly, these questions relate directly to the classic complaints about sales meetings.

The good news is that a coach can eliminate or at least control these problems and maximize the benefits of team meetings—especially the one special benefit: team building. Coaches can do this by applying the *skills* and *framework* for group coaching.

Meeting Skills

Coaching teams requires the same fundamental skills as coaching individuals.

- *Presence.* Provide leadership for the meeting without dominating it.

- *Rapport.* Take the time to "meet and greet" and recognize all members of the team.

- *Questioning.* Create a group dialogue by asking "Why do you feel that way?" "What do you think we can do?" "What are other points of view?" to find out the group's perspective before giving them your perspective.

- *Listening.* Show that you care about your salespeople, their ideas, their point of view. Avoid interrupting team members.

- *Positioning.* Comment on what a salesperson has said. Position your ideas to the needs of the group.

- *Checking.* Ask others for their views. Encourage a dialogue. Bring closure to agenda items.

But these skills must be used in the context of meeting tactics: One coach was so excited by his new-found skill when he learned how to run an effective sales meeting that he said, "I think with these tactics I can take over a small country." Another coach almost did. He applied his sales meeting skills and tactics at a meeting of his condo association and was elected its new president!

Meeting Tactics

Using these, the coach can lead effective team meetings.

Preparation

A good meeting starts with preparation. First, set your objective. If the coach isn't clear about the objectives and purpose of the meeting, it is unlikely that anyone else will be either, or that the meeting will be productive. Having an objective is step one—and often a step that is missing. The meeting can have an overall objective, but it helps to have an objective for each agenda item that specifies an output. And step two, which can put the "Why are we here?" complaint to rest, is communicating the objectives to participants at the start of the meeting. Having an agenda is a simple way to do this.

The Agenda

The *agenda*—a simple, written, 1-page agenda—is indispensable for *every* sales meeting. The best way to make sure you have objectives and that your objectives are expressed clearly is to prepare an agenda. Ideally, this is not a bunch of scribbles on a scrap of paper that the coach hoards, but a simple point-by-point list on a sheet of paper or a flip chart shared with the team members. The number of topics can be determined by the time frame for the meeting and the complexity of the points to be covered.

If nothing else, the agenda will make the purpose of the meeting clear. Getting the group committed to the meeting and the points to be covered is another matter entirely. But there is a process to use in *putting the agenda* together that can help build commitment and ownership.

Not surprisingly, the best way to get commitment to agenda items is to give salespeople an opportunity to impact the meeting by asking them what topics, issues, products, etc. are important to them. The time to do this, otherwise it probably won't happen, is at the *end* of the current meeting. Quickly, the coach and team can jointly develop all or part of the agenda for the *next* sales meeting. A comment like, "Let's set the agenda for our next meeting on (date). What are our priorities?" is useful. The coach can also invite team members to add agenda items up to several days before the meeting.

As a rule of thumb, the coach should contribute only a portion of the agenda. Salespeople who see that their ideas get on the next meeting's agenda usually are on board too. Of course, the coach can use his or her judgment to make sure the meeting focuses on priorities. For example, he or she can delay a suggested topic or deal with a particular subject in a one-on-one meeting or in a subgroup. But if topics that are *always* important to the salesforce are *never* important to the coach, something is off. The meeting agenda is a *powerful* tool not only to help keep the meeting on track, but also to build commitment and clarity of purpose. The power of the agenda depends in large part on *how it is used*. Here are some points to keep in mind.

Using the Agenda. An agenda should be distributed at the beginning of each meeting, after a few minutes of rapport and settling in. It is also OK to distribute an "advance" copy prior to the meeting, but since many of the topics would have been jointly developed, this may not really be necessary.

Touring the Agenda. Once the agenda has been given out, the coach should quickly "tour" (review) it, making no additional comments on any points at this time. The goal of the tour is to *headline* each topic and then check.

Checking the Agenda. Once the tour is complete, the coach should check for agreement by asking, "Are there any questions or concerns about the agenda?" This check gives people a chance to voice concerns. Someone may ask, "Why are we covering X when we need to do Y?" When this happens, the coach has several choices:

- Add the point to the agenda. (Be careful here. Remember, the agenda was jointly set, and people had the opportunity to add to it.)
- Table the point to another time and stick to the agenda.
- Set a time to deal with the point later—either one-on-one at another meeting or in another forum.

Having set the agenda with the team, the coach probably will have to limit the number of new topics that can be added. *How* the coach handles this is important.

Guarding the Agenda.   The coach's role is to be the guardian of the agenda. Only for a very compelling reason should the meeting be diverted from its original goals. The coach could say, "Let's start with the first topic. Since we have X topics to cover, and this is a key one, we should plan on spending about 20 minutes on this." And later the coach can say, "We have X and Y to cover yet; let's move on to...."

When a salesperson does go off track or onto a tangent, the coach can use the agenda to help the group stay focused. Like a goalie in ice hockey, coaches must keep their eyes on the topics being discussed and *not* let other topics slip in or take over. A comment like, "Tom, that's an important point. We are on X topic and we need to complete [objective]. So can we hold that until...? Let's go back to.... We can get to that point (the next agenda, possibly at the end of this meeting if there is time, or at another appropriate time)."

The coach is the guardian of the agenda and the agenda helps the coach set a focus and make headway. As mentioned earlier, describing each agenda item as an objective that includes a desired outcome can also be helpful. For example, if "offsetting X competition" is an agenda topic, it could be expressed as "to develop two or three strategies for positioning against X competitor."

Leveraging the Agenda.   It is up to the coach to leverage the power of the agenda. He or she should close on each agenda item before moving to the next one by asking, "What action can we take?" or "What have we decided?" And then coaches must make sure that that decision makes it to the decision minutes (discussed next). As an aside, I learned the value of closure to agenda items many years ago when I was a principal of a New York City high school. At each staff meeting *for several months* we discussed again and again the topic of student lateness. Finally, at one meeting, a teacher said, "We've discussed this 100 times. Let's either decide something concrete or drop the subject." Her comment startled all of us. We broke into three teams and each one presented a recommendation. We picked one: stop serving breakfast (rolls, milk) at 8:55 a.m. Our lateness problem corrected itself 80 percent in less than one week! More significant than the fact that we came up with an effective solution was our bent toward action. If our plan didn't work, we could have tried something else—and we would have, since we had begun taking action steps toward solving the problem. We had begun to build momentum!

Once the decision or action is set, be sure to *check*— "Before we move on...any questions...let's summarize what has been decided." After checking, the group can move on to the next item.

Decision Minutes

Decision minutes are not the ordinary (tedious) "minutes" of a meeting which give a blow-by-blow account of everything that transpired. They summarize decisions (action steps) committed to by the group, specifying who is responsible for the action step (accountability) and by when (time frame). Decision minutes become the "To Do" bible not only for the coach, but for all team members. They can usually be recorded on one page. A typical format can look like Figure 8-1.

The coach can be the one to write out decision minutes for the *first* meeting, but to help establish shared responsibility for each subsequent meeting, he or she can ask for volunteers, rotating the role of recording decision minutes for every meeting.

Decision minutes reflect the output of the agenda. At the end of each agenda item, the person recording the decision minutes

		Date: _____	
DECISION MINUTES			
Decision	Accountability	Time Frame	Follow-up/results

Figure 8-1 Decision minutes format.

should read the last decision. The coach should say, "Let's summarize what we are going to do, who will do it, and by when."

Having each decision in writing and backed by a commitment to the group by the person accountable increases group ownership and personal responsibility. Of course, deciding on an action step in a group and actually having something happen are two different things. Decision minutes are a great tool to *help* get things done, but they do not guarantee it. The coach must follow up.

Follow-up is the coach's main job after the meeting. That is why the coach's name should stay out of the accountability column. Too many coaches delegate to themselves. By keeping their names out of column two, they can follow up and provide support for their people.

Decision minutes should be completed *during* every meeting— if there are no decisions or next steps, it is unlikely the meeting was very productive.

Group Participation

Because of culture, role models, and skill level, most group meetings are not participatory. There is very little give and take. Rather than *interact,* in most sales meetings, the sales manager *acts.* He or she is *"on stage,"* rather than *"in sync," telling* rather than *teaming.* In most sales meetings, mangers *tell;* they do not *ask.*

Getting group participation begins with understanding roles: the role of the coach and the roles of the other participants. Initially, the coach should lead the sales meeting, but with strong team meeting skills, the coach can help the group become more responsible for the quality and productivity of the meetings.

Let's look at key participation skills and tactics.

Meetings by Questioning.   Perhaps the most important skill for creating group participation is questioning:

- *Ask open-ended questions.* Questions that begin with words like *what, why,* and *how,* help salespeople express and think through their ideas. For example, in discussing a prospecting phone blitz, instead of telling everyone how to handle gatekeepers, the coach can ask, "What are some things you do to get past and/or win over the gatekeepers?" Other examples are: *"What* has been your experience in calling clients to discuss...?" *"How* did you determine whether...?" By avoiding yes-or-no questions, questions that begin with *do* and *are,* the coach can foster interaction.

- *Volley questions.* Salespeople in meetings usually direct their questions to the coach. It is the coach's job to channel the question back to the group, rather than give the answer himself or herself. For example, the coach can say, "I am glad you brought that up. That objection can be tough. How are some of you dealing with it?" And when someone responds, ask the group to critique the *strengths* and areas for improvement.

- *Keep asking for other views.* After asking a question like "What have you experienced while dealing with...?" and having gotten an answer, the coach should not stop there. Other ideas are waiting to be expressed. By asking others for their view too— "What about someone else, what have others of you found?"— the coach can stimulate a productive dialogue.

- *Ask why .* Once team member ideas are on the table, the coach can go deeper by asking, "Why is that?"

- *Refrain from immediate judgment.* One of the worst things a coach can do is ask for input and immediately shoot it down. When a salesperson offers a suggestion that the coach does not think is feasible, he or she can handle this in several ways:

- Rather than reject ideas in an offhanded way, the coach can ask for the person's thinking.
- Get input from others, "How do you think that would work?"
- Make a comment of acknowledgment and then use the classic union leader technique of asking if there is another point of view—"Who has a different point of view?" Invariably someone will!

Even if a point is way off track, especially because of the group setting, a coach should refrain from saying, "No, that's ridiculous…," or he or she can alienate the contributor and discourage the entire group. Even in an open team environment, no one wants to "lose face."

If someone offers an idea that does not make sense, the coach can acknowledge the point, explore it, and reshape it as necessary. One good way to acknowledge a point is to say, "Tim, I am not sure I follow that, can you…," or, "How then would…?" Or, if something is just taking too much time, the coach can say, "Tim, perhaps we can discuss that after the meeting," or, "Let's hear from someone who has not spoken up yet." It is important not to let a team meeting turn into a one-on-one.

The key is ask and not tell to encourage salespeople to think and take responsibility for their learning.

Don't Ignore and Don't Interrupt.   It is important not to ignore or interrupt. One manager was shocked to see how often he did both when he saw a video of himself during a sales meeting. He not only had a habit of interrupting, but when he waited until someone was finished speaking, he would totally ignore what the person said and make his point, which was totally unrelated to what was just said.

Ask for Volunteers.   A coach doesn't have to call on people to get participation. "Drafting" people puts them on the spot, and most people resent it. Moreover, calling on salespeople sets the expectation that the coach will take initiative. Salespeople who are given a chance to participate voluntarily usually do so willingly and enthusiastically. By giving salespeople a chance to volunteer, the coach can make them feel respected and can reduce defensiveness.

There is a way to ask for volunteers and get them. Once the coach asks for a volunteer, he or she should use body language (head straight, not tilted, posture straight, wait silently) to show she or he expects participation. If someone doesn't volunteer, it is the coach's choice to keep waiting, ask why only one is participating, or simply call on a friendly face. A coach who *expects* participation can get it.

Tell Salespeople What You Expect.   A coach should clearly set the expectation that he or she wants participation. But unless the coach responds positively to input, salespeople will quickly clam up, thinking, "Why bother?"

It is also very important to be clear about how certain decisions will be made. For example, the coach may want *input* on how to handle leads but the coach may be the final decider in this area or he or she might want the group to decide. It is vital to make the boundaries clear or risk frustrating the group.

Listen.   The coach's ability to listen will help determine how much participation there is. Most coaches would be astounded to see how much they talk during a meeting and how little their people participate. The coach should role-model good listening skills: eye contact, comments of acknowledgment, questions, and so on.

Give and Encourage Feedback.   The coach has a perfect opportunity in a sales meeting to role-model feedback, whether the feedback is positive or critical. Using the fundamentals of one-on-one feedback, the coach can demonstrate for others the power of feedback:

- Listen

- Ask questions for clarification

- Find common ground

- Give feedback—*both* positives and areas for improvement

- Encourage others to give feedback

- Be honest and open; don't be brutal, particularly because it is in a group session

- Ask for feedback in return

Most important, the coach should hold off on giving his or her feedback and encourage others to give theirs first. The coach can do this by commenting or building on what people say, such as, "That's an important perspective," or, "John's idea that...How do others of you...?"

Network/Politic. When the coach is about to face a hot issue that is likely to stir the group, rather than go in cold, he or she can go to a few of his or her key people to feel them out and marshall their support.

Sensitivity. Because it is a group situation, it is important for the coach to be sensitive in what he or she says. The golden rule for group meetings is *don't cause anyone to lose face—ever!*

Participation Techniques

Here are some other ways to encourage involvement during a group sales meeting.

Clockwise. To help get a quiet group talking, try what is called in training jargon "round robin." This is a technique of asking for one volunteer and then going around the room clockwise to get input from all group members. Example: "Great, John will begin. Then let's go clockwise around the room to hear from all of you."

Role Play. Have salespeople role-play problems, challenges, and opportunities. Ask for volunteers to role-play a problem or situation as the group observes. Stop the process every few minutes to coach and help. The role play should be a way to improve, not to test; to develop, not evaluate.

Role playing is very powerful. It is one thing to *talk* about how to do something and another thing to actually do it. Rather than just discuss a problem, the coach can get the group to act it out informally. The coach can say, "Who will be that client for one minute? Just stay in your own seat. Who wants to deal with this issue as the salesperson for a few minutes?" The coach should then ask the group to critique the strengths and areas for improvement.

If one of the role-play participants runs into difficulty, take a "time out" to discuss what to do and then go back into the role play. If someone gets stuck, swap roles.

Rotating Accountability for Decision Minutes. For each meeting, a different person—including the coach—should record decision minutes as they are made. The recorder should jot down each decision as it is made and read it aloud before the group moves on to the next agenda topic. Almost everyone will be surprised to see how often the decision has to be reworded until everyone is in agreement about what was decided.

Debrief the Meeting. At the end of each sales meeting, the coach should ask for and encourage honest feedback on the meeting itself by asking each participant to identify a positive and negative of the meeting.

Most salespeople and coaches find this very difficult to do at first, but by asking for one positive and one negative from each salesperson, the coach gives permission for the group to criticize itself and the coach.

The key here is for the coach to *listen* to all comments and *not comment* as team members critique the meeting. The coach can take notes and then thank people for the feedback. Debriefing helps the salespeople become accountable for making the meetings better. The group can then use the critique to improve future meetings. One coach knew the process was working when a salesperson—not the coach—was the one who said, "I get here on time but have to wait every week for one or two people. If some of us can get here on time, all of us can." True development at coaching is not a one-coach concept. Peer feedback is powerful too.

Debriefing comments like these can be invaluable to making future meetings better and better:

- "It broke the ice. Now I feel I can call him. Having the specialist come in and talk with us was great. We need more of that!"

- "I wish we had gotten this booklet on his products ahead of time so I could have prepared."

- "Practicing how to find out from our clients who else they use was very helpful. In the past I have felt uncomfortable asking questions about the competition."

- "The cookies were a nice touch. Thanks!"

- "I really wish people would make a point of getting here on time. It's not fair that those of us who do get here have to wait."

- "Can we change rooms? This room is always too hot."

- "Can we change the time?"

Debriefing helps the group assume responsibility for the successes and failures of the meeting rather than leave all the burden on the coach. The coach can role-model how to receive feedback—listen, take notes, get all the feedback and not interrupt or discuss any point until all the feedback has been given, thank the group, and figure out how to use the ideas.

Interpersonal Factors

As mentioned several times in this book, the coach needs to be sensitive to what is said in any "public" forum (including a small group meeting) so that team members don't feel as though they have lost face. As the team becomes more open and more ready for group feedback, the discussions can become more open, too. However, topics that are very specific or personal to one person should always be handled one-on-one.

When a salesperson is acting hostile or rude to the coach or another salesperson, it is usually wise for the coach to refrain from using his or her authority in public. Everyone knows the coach has rank; there is no need to pull it. A simple comment like, "Bill, I think it is inappropriate to continue this discussion now. See me at the end of the meeting," can remove the problem from a public forum and *add* to the coach's credibility. By contrast, when one salesperson personally attacks another, it is the coach's role to model and intervene with a comment like, "Let's stick to issues, not people." In any event, it is best to move all interpersonal problems out of the group forum and put them behind closed doors unless the team has really reached the level of partnership.

Logistics

Even the best sales meeting skills can be lost if logistics are awry.

Time.   At a minimum, set the date for the next meeting at the end of the current meeting. Better yet, establish a preset schedule.

Depending on the situation this can be weekly (ideally), monthly, or, at minimum, quarterly meetings. In addition to knowing in advance the schedule for the meeting, a time slot should be set. It's not unusual to ask managers or salespeople what time an upcoming meeting will end and find out they have no idea! "Until the issue(s) is settled," is a common answer. *Wrong!* Productive meetings have sharp time limits—and they start and end on time. Meetings are not marathons. Meetings demand punctuality, and this starts with the *coach* being on time—starting on time and ending on time.

One coach says he cured his group's lateness problem by starting his meeting alone; he was already talking as the first person paraded in. It is also important to keep to the schedule and not cancel meetings unless circumstances truly warrant it. The coach's *behavior,* not his or her words, will set the standard and tell people how important—or unimportant—meetings are.

One hour per month is a minimum for a sales team and a minimum of one-half to one day a quarter is a recommendation for most teams. It can also be helpful to time agenda items, giving 5 to 30 minutes per item. Comments like, "We have 15 minutes left. So for the next ten minutes....Then we will debrief and set our next agenda."

Place. If possible, meetings should be held in a place away from phones and other interruptions. A conference room setting is ideal, since it gets the coach out from behind his or her desk and sitting *among* team members. For the true leader, there is no risk in this. After all, as the old Scottish saying goes, "Wherever McTavish sits is the head of the table." The coach should be sensitive to seating and not allow empty seats between participants or allow participants to sit outside of the group—"Please join in (move up/in) to help us be a more cohesive group."

If for geographic reasons the team cannot get together, the coach should use remote coaching alternatives such as conference phone calls.

Group Size.   Two to three or more people together constitute a meeting. Coaches can usually work best with groups of six to eight, but groups as small as three and as large as twenty or larger can be interactive, too.

Atmosphere.   The coach can help set a positive atmosphere by making refreshments available—for example, coffee, tea, juice, and danish for a 7:30 a.m. meeting and pizza for a 7:00 p.m. meeting.

One-on-one coaching that leads to individual improvement of course is great. A sales meeting that leads to greater teamwork can be even better. One is addition, the other is multiplication. Both are needed. The ever-expanding results easily pay for the time and effort the coach and team invest. Sales is a tough job, and sales meetings, when they are effective, provide much needed support to the players.

Sales meetings are a place to train, practice, critique, develop, and showcase. Teams can celebrate successes, dissect failures, plan strategies, and evaluate results. Most important, sales meetings are the place to build a high-performance team. The coach who can lead effective sales meetings can use the team meeting to build the team and create a peer coaching environment.

Peer Coaching

When an organization coaches peer-to-peer, not only manager-to-salesperson, it has a tremendous advantage. There is simply too much to do and too much to learn to rely on manager-salesperson feedback. The trend toward the flat organization has made self-coaching and peer-coaching skills essential. One *Fortune* 500 company we know has 28 district managers for 2,100 sales reps. Fortunately for them and organizations like them, developmental coaching is not a one-coach concept.

Many organizations are struggling to find a way to leverage all their resources to maintain and penetrate relationships. To do this, many are organizing around teams. But even with team training, most organizations find that the teams are not coming together as they had hoped. They are finding that there are teams *in structure,* and there are teams *in behavior.* The big difference is that in a well-functioning team—a team in behavior—the work of the team is more important than any one team member's agenda or ego.

Earlier in this book, we looked on "team-call coaching" (preparation for a team call) and at "coaching the team" (coaching at sales meetings). This section looks at peer feedback.

Teams that are teams in structure only are like a fish net. Teams that are teams in behavior are like a piece of burlap. The level and quality of feedback is a key determiner of how tight the weave is. If the feedback is open and honest—and of course the intent is to help—the weave is close and the team is close.

The ultimate in coaching is peer coaching. The best coaches coach as a peer—receiving as well as giving feedback. As mentioned earlier, the coach must inspire trust and be a role model for feedback. If the coach does not give and, even more important, ask for feedback, it is fairly safe to say the peers in his or her group will not give each other feedback or readily accept it either.

Peer coaching is not a session. It is a culture. A coach that can foster feedback among his or her team—person-to-person—can create a team that can proactively coach itself. When this happens, coaching happens during the action, on the run, every day.

The key to this is for the coach to ask for feedback for him or herself directly and for the organization. Again, the good news is that peer coaching can begin with the individual coach. Those who want to encourage peer feedback can do so—even without management, evaluation, and compensation systems to support it (although if the coach can influence such systems, this is certainly the way to go).

Even with the coach as a role model for giving and receiving feedback, peer-to-peer coaching can be difficult. The peer doing the coaching may be younger or may be making less money than the peer he or she is coaching.

Salespeople generally acknowledge that it is appropriate for the manager/coach to give feedback to those "under" him or her. They say this because the coach is often more experienced, more knowledgeable, and in a "higher" position than they are. And most managers at least assume that feedback is a part of their jobs. No such assumption exists in peer-to-peer situations. "Subordinates" assume it is the job of the "boss." Honest peer-to-peer talk in many organizations is taboo.

As organizations change, this taboo is being challenged. In the traditional definition, level and title defines who is a peer. For teams to flourish, the tasks and the dynamics between individuals, not titles or structures, must be the factors that determine who is a peer. For peer coaching to work, all team members—in the broadest sense of the term—must be peers.

The implicit "contract" peers make with one another is that they will help each other get better. Key to this is giving one another open and honest feedback, particularly in team selling situations. Sales teams are usually made up of various levels and functions. Therefore, it makes no sense to limit the feedback to the manager role. In general, peers have more contact with one another than with their managers. In team selling situations peers often have more data about each other than the managers.

360-degree feedback includes peer feedback, but keep in mind that this is evaluative and often written. It does not replace developmental peer feedback. Ongoing verbal developmental feedback is the path to improvement.

All organizations generate valuable information about people: above, across, and below. It is important to include feedback from above and below, but it is even more important to understand that the richest source of information by far is the peer group. Peer coaching can be the most valuable because the people who know the most about someone are not his or her "bosses" or even the coaches, but the person's peers.

When one-on-one peer coaching is working, something else can happen—the peer group can begin to do group peer coaching. The coach is often the one to encourage and role-model this. Peer coaching can happen coach-to-salesperson, salesperson-to-coach, salesperson-to-salesperson, division-to-division, and unit-to-unit. The crowning achievement is reached when an organization achieves a sense of true organizationwide partnership. Then the organization is positioned to develop true client partnerships. By overcoming its silo problem, an organization can leverage its resources.

Three Stages

Let's look at the three stages of peer coaching.

Stage One

The first stage of peer coaching occurs between two colleagues who view each other as peers and agree to coach each other. A good example of this is a friendship, which, as everyone knows, can be a powerful force for positive change. In-depth coaching on an individual's obstacle should always be one-on-one.

Stage Two

The next stage is a larger group of people (three or more) who have contact with each other and have made an agreement to coach each other. The coaching and feedback usually begin as private (one-on-one) and end up being public (in front of other team members)—unless the feedback is very specific to one person.

The benefits of "public" peer coaching can be tremendous, when a team is ready for it. For example, when a teammate shouts to a batter who is about to face a wild pitcher "lay off the high ones," this can help other players as well. Offered and accepted in a spirit of trust and teamwork, feedback can help both individuals and teams move to their next level of excellence.

Stage Three

The next and most difficult stage in peer coaching is organizational coaching. This occurs when an entire organization embraces peer coaching. In this kind of culture, feedback is not viewed as a personal threat. Instead it is taken as an opportunity for improvement. To assess how close to it (or how far from it) your organization is, here are six questions:

- Does your organization encourage coaching? *This is a good beginning.*

- Do managers actually coach? *The more the better (although remember, change can start with just one).*

- Is the coaching developmental or evaluative? *The more the balance is toward developmental coaching, the greater the learning and the more the organization is moving toward becoming a learning culture.*

- Is the coaching nonhierarchical? *Is it just the "bosses" who coach or is there also peer coaching? Ideally manager coaching evolves into peer coaching.*

- What is the quality of the coaching? *It should be positive, open, and honest.*

- Is the environment of the organization one of fear or support? *Fear hampers development; support fosters it.*

Overview of Peer Coaching

The process of peer coaching is based on the developmental coaching model. In peer coaching, peer A should first give his or her ideas, for example, before the call or assess his or her own performance or situation after a call and then ask for feedback from peer B. "Here's what I think. Here's how I think I did. My strengths....My areas for improvement....What do you see?" Or, "Here's how I handled this....What am I missing? What do you think?" Then B can challenge or question to come up with a better plan or give feedback on his or her performance/ideas/next steps and ask for feedback from A. The discussion ends with action steps.

While peer coaching uses the same developmental coaching process as does traditional coach/manager coaching, there are some slight differences. Peer coaching is much more like an invitation. Compare this example of traditional coaching versus peer coaching.

- *Coach to salesperson:* "How about getting that to me in about two weeks?" (This may not be perfect, but it certainly is fine.)
- *Peer coach to peer:* "When do you think you can get that to me?" or "When do you think we can get back together on this?"

Peer coaching, without a doubt, is more challenging than traditional/managerial coaching. It requires a special effort, energy, and enthusiasm to keep the relationship mutual. It requires willingness to open up about oneself in front of others and a feeling that the competition is outside the organization, not inside. It requires two people committed to look at their own and each other's performance and proactively give each other feedback. One of the biggest dangers in peer coaching, since there is more directness, is that it can slip into a gripe session or escalate into sniping—or just get sidetracked. Another challenge is that the level of directness among peers is usually greater. Peers may hedge when they talk to their manager/coach, but they are usually much more direct peer to peer. The objections that are raised can be much tougher. If a peer feels he or she is being treated in a condescending way, he or she is apt to close off or become aggressive.

Also, when peers get together, the parties often share extremely detailed technical information which, although invaluable, can also cause them to focus on the technicals or begin to tell war stories. They can easily lose their developmental agenda and then become very frustrated with the lack of progress. Peers in fact do debrief, but it is on the deal, product, or customer, not their skills or strategy. Therefore, it is vital to be absolutely clear about the objective of the peer coaching session and to stick to it.

For peer coaching to work people must share a belief in the value of helping one another to get better. Their mutual deal is simple: *"I'll help you be as good as you can be and you'll help me in the same way."* Without mutual trust and commitment, people often become competitive and resentful, and the deal falls apart.

In peer coaching situations it is also very important for a person to avoid becoming a part of a triangle. When coaching as a peer, one should represent only one's own point of view and should take full ownership for what is said. When acting as the "message bearer" for a group, the peer coach must have the permission of the group members to represent them and should clearly articulate that permission as a part of the message.

Peer coaching needs to be mutual. It is a two-way street. Both people must give and get feedback. They should also maintain a positive, respectful attitude—not listening for what they disagree with, but what they can take away and use. See Figure 9-1 for peer feedback guidelines.

Manager as Peer

Without diminishing the role of the manager, a key goal of developmental coaching is to create peer relationships in the area of development. The manager remains a manager in the hierarchical, administrative, and technical sense, but he or she becomes a peer or team leader in a developmental sense.

Everyone has had the unfortunate experience of working with a "bad" manager. But everyone has had at least one wonderful experience (we hope) of working *with* a "good" manager. Most

---

Peer Coaching

- Get mutual agreement to coach each other.

- Set an objective for every session and stay focused on it.

- Engage in a peer conversation—don't be condescending or dictatorial.

- When encountering resistance, use the objection resolution model (please see Chapter 4).

- Set action steps mutually; don't impose them.

- Be honest.

- Be open. Be receptive.

- Coach privately, giving team feedback only when it is the norm and circumstances warrant it.

- Avoid gossip or hearsay.

- Make it a two-way street.

- Don't become a part of a triangle. Use "I," not "they," and "we" only with permission. As they say, "Speak for yourself." Remember, everyone is a potential peer.

- Use feedback skills—each person should give feedback on his or her self first and then ask for feedback to get around blind spots.

- End on an action step.

Figure 9-1   Guidelines for giving peer feedback.

often this relationship feels to both parties like a peer relationship. In those relationships, there is mutual trust and professional and personal respect. Any salesperson working in this environment knows that working with such a manager "feels" like working with a peer. When the manager's interest is truly in the growth and development of a person *and* when the manager has good coaching skills, the relationship between the two feels "peer."

Managers in this role not only give feedback in a developmental way but are open to feedback, soliciting it frequently as a way to strengthen their own skills as well as the relationship with their people. (See Figure 9-2 on page 154 for a sample peer coaching critique form.)

In summary, the fundamental ideal of peer coaching is that one colleague agrees to help another and then receives help in return. What could be better?

Colleague 1: _____   Colleague 2: _____

Criteria	Strengths	Areas for Improvement
Preparation • Planning • Agreement to peer coach		
Peer Coaching Process • Colleague 1 assesses his/her own strengths and areas for improvement and then asks for feedback from Colleague 2. • Colleague 2 provides strengths and areas for improvement. Both colleagues problem-solve. (This process is then repeated for Colleague 2.) • Each colleague sets action steps.		
Mutual • Colleagues coach one another—two-way process.		
Quality of Developmental Feedback • Specific • Open, honest • Intent to help • Strengths and areas for improvement		
Team Effort • Partnership to get to the next level • Supportive		
Teamwork • Leads to improvement of strategy, skill, and relationship		

Figure 9-2   Peer coaching critique form.

Self-Coaching

One of the most common complaints that sales managers and senior management have regarding their salespeople is that they don't "take initiative." Interestingly enough, that is the same complaint many salespeople have about their managers and their senior management. Effective sales leadership and sales coaching cannot exist without initiative. What is initiative? It is people *willing* and *able* to take responsibility for their development.

For people to really self-coach they must be able to get excited (not fearful) about what they don't know. They need to see not knowing as an obstacle, not a failure. In a sense, to self-coach people must find the kid that is in all of us—the excitement of the unknown, the curiosity, the energy to learn. At the same time, people must have the stamina and discipline to convert these into useful knowledge and skills.

With self-coaching, salespeople learn how to take initiative and assume responsibility for their *own* learning and development. Self-coaching is the ultimate achievement because the person who can self-coach can be internally motivated and independent. The coach can be the role model for this if he or she teaches people how to internalize the developmental coaching process.

Companies often wonder why their initiatives aren't as effective as they hoped they would be. Perhaps they are sending one message and living another—talking Stretch Zone and living in the Comfort Zone.

Many companies today say they want their people to be "entrepreneurial" and flexible. They say they want "self-starters" and "risk takers." They spend money on creativity training to get such catalysts. The reality is that in many organizations, people who fit this description are viewed as mavericks. Unless they really produce fast, they can easily become unwelcome and seem like misfits to the culture. A company's words may support risk-taking but the reality may be that a short-term failure, far from being viewed as a learning experience, becomes punishment time.

The difference between a great coach and an OK coach is that the great coach can see failure as an opportunity. No one likes failure. And I am not talking about a pattern of failure. For a coach to really develop people, he or she must free him or herself up to self-develop and become the role model for self-coaching.

Self-coaching does not mean people are not taught or supported; it simply means they should take the initiative to seek the knowledge and support their needs.

Self-coaching takes time. People must stop the action and create the space, both mentally and physically, to think about their performance. This involves contemplating three questions:

- What did I do well?
- What are my areas for improvement?
- Where can I go to learn more?

The third question is *vital,* since it leads to new information and new perspectives. As stated earlier, everyone has blind spots, and the third question provides a channel for outside perspectives and information. This is the point at which an environment of peer coaching becomes invaluable. As mentioned throughout the book, most people will not seek feedback and will not be open to feedback in an environment of fear. But in a supportive environment where there is a coaching value—a continuous learning culture—people can and will self-coach and seek feedback.

In looking at performance, the sales critique checklist in the Appendix can be helpful. But a salesperson cannot do it all alone: He or she needs an outside view.

Self-coaching is a journey to mastery. One coach was on the right track when he said, "I tell my people that we are busy. I'm here. I'll get to them. But it is also up to them to ask for feedback from me and others and not wait for their evaluation to see how they are doing."

This coach is helping put development where it needs to be—in the hands of his salespeople. People are responsible for their own development; coaches should be there to support this. Developmental coaching lends to peer coaching and peer coaching lends to self-coaching.

A wonderful artist, art collector, and builder, Ian Woodner, once said he was his own best model for his painting. Why? Because the artist and model got tired at the same time. Similarly, the best coach can be the self-coach—always there and seeing what was strong and what could be improved.

Epilogue

More than 20 years ago when I was a principal of a New York City high school, nothing told more about what was going on in a school than its corridors. Based on the past 19 years of working with the leading organizations in the world, I see coaching in the same way. Nothing tells more about the management and culture of an organization than whether real coaching and feedback go on. And just as most of the inner city school corridors were/are in bad shape, so is the state of coaching in most organizations—if it exists at all.

The sad part of all this is that most salespeople have innate ability and integrity. But they also require support. They need feedback. If they don't get it, they will invent it. Without feedback, they won't improve or go deeper into their sales effectiveness. Without feedback they will have no real teamwork and no lasting victory. And they need to be made responsible for their own development.

The developmental coaching approach covered in this book is not a set of techniques. It is a way of life for the coach, the team, and the organization. Once open and honest feedback is a part of the culture, an organization with the basics is almost assured of success. It is in the Stretch Zone.

Coaching builds skills and it builds relationships. It is a way to help salespeople become more productive, more creative, and better at what they do—better in their strategy, their skills, their client and internal relationships, and their attitudes. Through coaching a coach can send a critical message—"We are good now; we can be even better." It is truly a leap—continuously working to get to the next level and the level beyond that.

Organizations that want to develop training programs that have real impact must worry more about what goes on outside the seminar room than in the seminar room. The most effective training happens in the coaching "corridor" where people ask each other: What did we do well? What can we do better? Where can we go to learn more?

You can begin by asking the first question. Start by asking for feedback yourself. Listen. Be open. Be willing to change. Do something differently. Make the leap from boss to coach today.

Coaching Tools

Following are some worksheets to help the manager improve coaching skills.

- Coach's Self-Critique
- Consultative Coaching Model
- Peer Developmental Coaching Critique
- Coaching Self-Assessment Quiz
- Coaching Planner
- Coach's Worksheet for Follow-up Analysis
- Guidelines for Giving and Receiving Feedback
- Sales Critique Checklist
- Sales Call Planner
- Team Call Planner

Coach's Self-Critique

	Strengths and Areas for Improvement

Developmental Coaching Framework
 	
• Preparation
  – Set clear objective
• Open
  – Build rapport
  – State purpose
• Perceptions/Needs
  – Get salesperson's perceptions first
  – State common ground
  – Give your perceptions
  – Check perceptions/agree to obstacles
• Identify and Remove Obstacles
  – Have two-way discussion
  – Question for obstacle
  – Ask salesperson for desired outcome
  – Ask salesperson to suggest options/ideas
  – Practice demonstrate
  – Ask salesperson to suggest solution
• Close/Action Step
  – Mutually agree on plan of action
  – Set at least one developmental step
  – Set measurable action step
    and time frame for follow-up
  – Cheerlead/encourage
• Follow-up	

Feedback • Balance strengths/areas for improvement • Limit your feedback • Be specific • Be honest • Be timely	
Attitude • Be helpful/positive • Be nonjudgmental • Primarily developmental, not evaluative feedback	
Six Critical Skills • Presence • Rapport • Questioning • Listening • Positioning • Checking	
Results of Coaching Session • Did you meet your objective? • Is there mutual satisfaction with outcome? • Is relationship improved?	

Figure A-1

Consultative Coaching Model—Six-Step Checklist

Preparation
- Set objective before the session. What do you want to see as the desired outcome?

Open
- Set the stage/environment.
- Build rapport and state your purpose.

Perceptions/Needs
- Ask for the salesperson's perception before stating yours.
- Ask for both strengths and areas for improvement.
- Ask what and why.
- Reiterate where you agree.
- State your perceptions by giving feedback on both strengths and areas for improvement as you see the situation.

Identify and Remove Obstacles
- Check to see if there is an agreement on the obstacle/performance issue, opportunity, or problem—and check level of severity.
- Remove obstacles.
- Ask salesperson for desired outcome.
- Ask salesperson for options/ideas.
- Stay focused on the issue, not the person.
- Focus on only one to three (at most) areas.
- Encourage problem-solving dialogue. Practice, demonstrate, role-play if appropriate.
- Build the working relationship/partnership.
- Let the salesperson suggest the mutually acceptable solution.

Close/Action Step
- Ask the salesperson to summarize agreement.
- Decide on at least one specific developmental step with time frames.
- Set the follow-up action and time.
- Cheerlead by giving words of encouragement.
- Consider asking for feedback.

Follow-up
- Monitor the salesperson's progress.
- Review your notes before the next coaching session.
- Evaluate results/improvement.

Figure A-2

Peer Developmental Coaching Critique

Criteria	Strengths	Areas for Improvement
Preparation • Planning • Agreement to peer coach		
Peer Coaching Process • Colleague 1 first assessed his or her *own* strengths and areas for improvement and then asked for feedback from Colleague 2 • Each colleague asked questions to help the other colleague identify and remove the obstacle • Each colleague gave feedback, solved problems, and set action steps		
Mutual • Colleagues coached one another — two-way process		
Quality of Feedback • Open, honest • Strengths and areas for improvement • Intent to help • Specific, limited		
Team Effort • Forming a partnership • Supportive		
Teamwork • Improvement of skill and approach • Strengthening of the relationship		

Figure A-3

Coaching Self-Assessment Quiz

Coach: _____	Date: _____				
How would you describe the coaching you provide?		**Poor**	**Fair**	**Good**	**Very Good**	**Excellent**

	Poor	Fair	Good	Very Good	Excellent
• Quality of your coaching	1	2	3	4	5
• Frequency of your coaching	1	2	3	4	5
• Helpfulness of your coaching	1	2	3	4	5
• Timeliness/appropriateness in time and place	1	2	3	4	5
• Use of achievable objectives	1	2	3	4	5
• Use of specific behavioral feedback	1	2	3	4	5
• Use of praise	1	2	3	4	5
• Setting of an action step	1	2	3	4	5
• Following up	1	2	3	4	5
• Your openness to receiving feedback	1	2	3	4	5
• Your use of praise/celebration of successes	1	2	3	4	5

1. To what extent do you think the people you coach would agree with the above assessment of your coaching effectiveness? ____ somewhat ____ very much ____ not at all

2. To what extent is your coaching balanced — positive and areas for improvement? ____ always ____ sometimes ____ never

3. What percentage of your coaching is proactive (planned/unsolicited)? ____ %

4. What percentage is on the spot (reacting to something that happened)? ____ %

5. What percentage is developmental (versus evaluative)? ____ %

6. How likely is it that individuals you work with would seek/initiate coaching and feedback from you? ____ somewhat ____ very much ____ not at all

7. What percentage of your time do you spend coaching (versus doing)? ____ % coaching ____ % doing

8. When you coach, do you let the other person talk first and give his or her perceptions before you give yours? ____ always ____ sometimes ____ never

9. In a coaching session, do you ask the person being coached to suggest the solution? ____ always ____ sometimes ____ never

10. At each coaching session, is there a clear understanding of what is expected and at least one clear developmental action step to work on, with time frame? ____ always ____ sometimes ____ never

11. Do you follow up consistently to monitor progress, results, and improvement? ____ always ____ sometimes ____ never

12. Do you make sure you consistently reward/recognize performance? ____ always ____ sometimes ____ never

13. How do you view your developmental sales coaching job compared with your other responsibilities? ____ as important ____ more important ____ less important

14. To what extent do you ask for feedback? ____ always ____ sometimes ____ never

Figure A-4

Coaching Planner

Salesperson: _____ Date: _____

Identify the coaching issue/problem/situation:

Key areas for growth:

Key strengths:

What is the objective of your coaching session?

What level of commitment/cooperation or resistance do you anticipate?

What specific behaviors/examples are you able to give feedback on (strengths/areas for improvement)?

What objections do you anticipate? How valid are they? How will you resolve them?

What questions will you ask?

What will you do to help this individual improve?

What is the desired action step?

Figure A-5

Coach's Worksheet for Follow-up Analysis

If you are dissatisfied with the results of a coaching session or would like to assess your coaching skills, use this form to describe the coaching situation and your response.

Coaching situation

_____

_____

_____

How did you handle the issue(s)?

_____

_____

_____

_____

What were the results?

_____

_____

_____

_____

What specific developmental steps can you take to improve your coaching effectiveness?

DEVELOPMENTAL STEPS	TIME FRAMES	COMPLETED
_____	_____	☐
_____	_____	☐
_____	_____	☐
_____	_____	☐
_____	_____	☐

Figure A-6

Guidelines for Giving and Receiving Feedback

Giving Feedback
- Be honest—always tell the truth. Do not be brutal.
- Be open.
- Focus on a *few* key points—know your objective. Limit feedback—don't overload.
- Be specific—stick to performance.
- Avoid value judgment.
- Be timely—give feedback as close to the event as possible.
  - If you or the person being coached are very upset, take time to calm down.
- Give strengths *and* areas for improvement.
- Give feedback specific to an individual in privacy.

Receiving Feedback
- Be open, receptive to learning.
  - Separate listening from judgment. Instead of listening for what you do not agree with, listen for something to learn and take away from the feedback.
  - Do not taint the validity of the message based on previous experiences or associations with the person giving feedback.
  - Recognize your defensiveness, accept it, and let it go.
- Don't interrupt. Get *all* your feedback.
- Don't defend.
- Listen actively.
  - Pay attention to body language and use body language.
  - Ask clarifying questions.
  - Take notes.
- Thank the giver.
- Reflect—consider the possibilities for development.
- Commit to doing something. Don't be passive.

As a Coach, Be Open to Feedback
- Invite others to give feedback to you.
- Ask, "What could I do differently to improve the situation?"

Figure A-7

Sales Critique Checklist

Criteria	Strengths and Areas for Improvement
Planning for the Sales Call • Homework	
Decision Makers/Influencers • Identification of decision-making unit • Influencers	
Opening/Introduction • Greeting, rapport; summary/hinge, positioning the call, bridging to needs	
Identification of Client's Needs • Identification of and response to client needs	
Positioning Product/Ideas • Knowledge of products/capabilities and benefits tailored to needs	
Questioning/Listening • Depth and range of questions • Questioning skills • Integration of client ideas/words	
Objections • Empathy/question/position/check	
Checking • Testing for understanding/agreement • Feedback, dialogue	
Action Step • Checking, next step, asking for business	
Six Critical Skills • Presence, rapport, questioning, listening, positioning, checking • Dialogue	
Competition • Identification of competitors, gaining information, offsetting competition	
Strategy • Game plan, resources	
Control • Salesperson's determined direction	
Nonverbal Behavior • Body language, idiosyncrasies	
Interpersonal Factors • Confidence/empathy/rapport	
Team • Roles, support, appropriate resources	
Objective/Close • Objectives met, next steps	

Figure A-8

Sales Call Planner

Relationship: _____ Contact: _____ Date: _____ Phone: _____ Fax: _____
Salesperson: _____ Team Member(s): _____

Sales Objective(s):	
Assumed Client Need(s):	
Decision Makers:	Your Team:
Main Issues from Last Contact/Present Situation:	
Ideas/Products/Services:	
Call Agenda Items:	
Questions:	
Objections:	
Competition:	
Closing:	
Next Steps:	
Internal cc:	

Figure A-9

Team Call Planner

Relationship: _____ Client/Prospect: _____
Salesperson: _____
Team: _____ Date: _____ Time: _____ to _____

Sales Objective(s):
Client Contacts:
Client Expectations and Needs:
Client Background:
Competitors:
Status of Relationship: *Issues/Priorities:*
Strategy:

Agenda:

Topic	*Team Member*	*Time*
_____	_____	_____
_____	_____	_____
_____	_____	_____

Key Questions:
Anticipated Objections:
Desired Action Step at Closing:
Internal cc:

Figure A-10

About the Author

Linda Richardson is president of The Richardson Company, sales training and management consultants to business, whose clients include Kimberly-Clark, AIG, Sony, Johnson and Johnson, Andersen Consulting, Price Waterhouse, and Citicorp. She teaches at the University of Pennsylvania's Wharton School and is the author of *Selling by Phone; Stop Telling, Start Selling;* and *Winning Group Sales Presentations.*

Additional information on The Richardson Company can be obtained by calling (215) 735-9255 or visiting its website at www.richardsonco.com.

Index